# Good
# Earth
# Art

# Good Earth Art

Environmental
Art
For
Kids

MaryAnn F. Kohl
Cindy Gainer

illustrations
Cindy Gainer

BRIGHT IDEAS FOR
LEARNING CENTERS

Bright Ring
Publishing

# CREDITS

**Typography: Digitype**
**Illustrations: Cindy Gainer**
**Cover Artist: Scott Montgomery**

ISBN 0-935607-01-3

Library of Congress Catalog Card Number: 91-71130

Manufactured in the United States of America

10   9

Published by
*BRIGHT RING PUBLISHING*
P.O. Box 5768
Bellingham, WA 98227

## Publisher's Cataloging in Publication
*(Prepared by Quality Books Inc.)*

Kohl, MaryAnn F.
   Good earth art : environmental art for kids / MaryAnn F. Kohl, Cindy Gainer ; illustrations Cindy Gainer.
   p. ill. cm. -- (Bright ideas for learning)
   Includes bibliographical references and index.
   ISBN 0-935607-01-3: $16.95

   1. Arts--Study and teaching. 2. Environment (Art)--United States --Study and teaching.   I. Gainer, Cynthia.  II. Title. III. Series.

NX280                    702
                              QBI91-1570

---
**ATTENTION: SCHOOLS AND BUSINESSES**
---

Bright Ring Publishing books are available for quantity discounts with bulk purchase for educational, business, or sales promotional use.

For information, please write to Bright Ring Publishing, P.O. Box 5768, Bellingham, WA 98227.

## DEDICATION:

To Michael, Hannah, and Megan with love and appreciation.

– M.A.K.

To Bill and August with love.

– C.G.

## ACKNOWLEDGEMENTS:

Special thanks to Cindy Gainer, my co-author, whose enthusiasm for writing and illustrating and knowledge of children's creative needs was an inspiration to my own creativity. Further thanks to Sarabeth Goodwin and Larry Rood at Gryphon House for their faith in me and their patience and advice. Thanks also to friends who constantly hold me up, send me new ideas, and keep me laughing: Kris Grinstad, Bonnie Stafford, Peggy Campbell, and Pat Asmundson. Special acknowledgement goes to my family who is the creative source of valuable input and keeps me pointed toward my vision, sorting out the best of the best to make this book happen. Thanks, everyone!

– M.A.K.

I would like to acknowledge MaryAnn Kohl for her open communication, genuine warmth and sincerity resulting in the creation of *Good Earth Art;* Sandy May for her computer resources; Jean Coursey for her helpful suggestions; and my family and friends for supporting my efforts.

– C.G.

# USING THE SYMBOLS

In the upper page margins and in the Table of Contents, graphic symbols can be found to make the projects in *Good Earth Art* usable and accessible. The symbols will help quickly identify which projects are appropriate for your particular needs. Use them as suggestions. Feel free to experiment and change projects to suit your needs, the needs of your children, and to utilize whatever supplies you have on hand.

 **Age Suggestion**
- indicates a general idea of age appropriateness. No two children are alike in ability or interest at any age, so use this symbol only as a suggestion and not a firm rule. The "+" means *all* ages above that number. A project labeled 1+up is truly that - for one year olds *on up to adult*. Let your knowledge of children guide you in selecting projects, and use this symbol as a loose indication of difficulty.

 **Recycled Materials**
- indicates projects that use materials saved from the trash or gathered from free sources. Most of these projects can be recycled after creating, or after they have been enjoyed for a period of time.

 **From Nature**
- indicates a project which uses materials collected from the backyard, woods, beach, or which takes place in the outdoors.

 **Good Group Project**
- these projects work especially well with large and small groups, as well as individual art exploration.

 **Edible**
- eat this project during use or at completion. Only eat projects with this symbol.

 **Homemade**
- indicates a project that is made to substitute for a commercial product.

 **Gift**
- indicates an art project which can be used as a gift, as a container for a gift, or as wrapping for a gift.

 **Supervision**
- indicates a project that needs help only in the preparation of materials *before beginning to create,* or is difficult and needs help throughout (especially in the case of young children).

**Caution**
- usually indicates that use of electrical or sharp tools is involved. Suggests taking extra care during a particular step of the project to avoid injury or mishap.

**Author's Favorite**
- indicates projects which each author has chosen as one of her favorite projects. Reasons for choice vary, but usually suggest the art activity is "fun," "pretty," or "good for the earth."

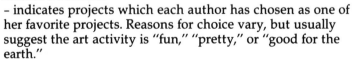
Bright Ring Publishing and the authors of *Good Earth Art* cannot be held responsible for injury, mishap, or damages incurred during the use of or because of art projects in *Good Earth Art.* The authors recommend appropriate and reasonable supervision at all times based on the age and capability of each child. Do not leave children unattended.

# TABLE OF CONTENTS

*See page 6 for Symbol Definitions.*

See page 6 for Symbol Definitions.

# 7 BUILDING BLOCKS TO CREATIVITY

1. **Self-Confidence**
   Respect a child's ideas and efforts. Allow the child to experience accomplishment by giving his creativity time and space, time to work out ideas, and by giving imagination a chance.

2. **Allow Non-Conformity**
   Let a child know that it's O.K. to listen to Thoreau's "different drummer". It is desirable to break away from what everyone else is doing.

3. **Explore and Think**
   Encourage a child to think a project through, but first allow exploration and experimentation without criticism. After experiencing materials and ideas, thought patterns and plans of action will fall into place.

4. **Exposure**
   Being introduced to new experiences, cultural events, games, and activities encourages original thinking and imagining. Provide materials for a child to explore with no particular outcome.

5. **Respect**
   A child should be encouraged to respect his own ideas and the ideas of those around him in order to develop new ideas. Watching a child too closely can be limiting, as can fostering competition or restricting choices. Praise freely and sincerely.

6. **Imagination Permission**
   Give permission to the child to embrace imagination freely without fear of criticism or outside control. People who do not feel comfortable being imaginative hold themselves back from creativity. Let imagining feel positive, and yes, even fun!

7. **Thinking in New Ways**
   Encourage thinking in new ways. Try new things. Experiment and explore and make mistakes. Learning from mistakes hands-on is the best teacher available to each child. Encourage the child to try the opposite way, the untraveled idea, the silly, or the unusual. Discoveries can be made daily!

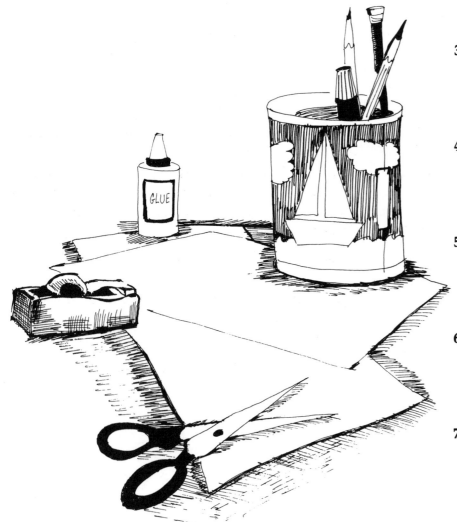

# INTRODUCTION

**Who uses *Good Earth Art*?**

*Good Earth Art* is a resource for all ages, young and old. Young children explore any project in the book no matter what the age suggestion, as long as they have appropriate help. Older children add maturity and experience to even the most basic project, and will find all projects a challenge or discovery even if the age suggested is younger than their own.

Adults using *Good Earth Art* will enjoy helping children select suitable projects based on the materials or supplies on hand, but will also enjoy using the art experiences for their own creative enjoyment. The authors do!

**What about saving materials?**

Everyone is encouraged to save and collect supplies rather than buying a product just to get to the resulting art material. Some products are not particularly sound for the environment, and their purchase is not recommended. However, when left-over plastics, papers, styrofoams, and other materials are found, saving and using them for art is better than simply throwing them in the trash. Making use of existing or left-over materials and product packaging is the goal rather than purchasing the product.

Schools and offices often have great amounts of throwaways that can be recycled into art. First look in the Index for suggested materials, and then start searching for those materials to save for art projects. You may never have to buy anything in order to do the projects in *Good Earth Art*, other than basic art supplies like paint and glue.

**What's special about *Good Earth Art*?**

The art experiences in *Good Earth Art* enable children to acquaint themselves with the natural qualities of the earth such as leaves, rocks, shells, dirt, wind, rain, and sunshine. Children also learn to observe, create, and remain in touch with our changing world, and to develop a caring attitude towards the earth by learning to recycle and use materials for art rather than throwing them away.

**Is it the process of creating or the finished product that matters in children's art?**

*Good Earth Art* encourages children to explore and create without worrying about the finished product. Children experiment, make mistakes, try new ideas of their own, and enjoy the thrill of the creative process. There is no right way or wrong way for projects to turn out, just the joyful pleasant process of the experience.

Given sufficient time for exploration and experimentation in art, children will refine their work automatically and independently. They will judge their own results and work towards their own goals, often with the most incredible, surprising results!

Explore. Experiment. Create. Enjoy the creative sparkle of each child.

From MaryAnn –
*"Imagination is more important than knowledge, for knowledge is limited, whereas imagination embraces the entire world."*
– Albert Einstein

From Cindy –
*"Art is not a thing, it is a way."*

– Albert Hubbard, 1911

# DRAWING AND PAINTING

chapter 1

# FREE DRAWING OR PAINTING

**MATERIALS:**
any paper
crayons, paints, pens, pencils
leaves, weeds, wildflowers

**PROCESS:**
1. Collect used paper with unusual textures, surfaces, and sizes.
   (Hint: Ask your local print shop to save a box for you. Sometimes they have foiled papers, sticker-backed paper, and unusual textures and sizes.)
2. Allow free drawing or painting to be stimulated by the uniqueness of the paper.

**EXTENSION:**
**nature's drawings**
1. Collect leaves, weeds, and wildflowers.
2. Use the collected items to draw with. Press, rub, or squeeze leaves or flowers into the paper to draw with their natural juices and colors.
3. Experiment with using juice from berries, too.

**VARIATIONS:**
**use unusual papers for —**
1. ink pad printing
2. vegetable prints
3. any project asking for paper

# NEWSPAPER DESIGN

**MATERIALS:**
paper
newspaper
tempera paint
paintbrush
scissors
crayons
paste or glue
extra newspaper to cover the table
water or a jar to wash out the brush

**PROCESS:**
1. Paint a background on the paper.
2. Set aside to dry.
3. Draw a design on the newspaper.
4. After the background has dried, paste or glue design onto it. Use crayons to add details, if desired.

**VARIATIONS:**
**Try —**
1. a dinosaur on jungle background
2. flowers on grass
3. boat on water
4. buildings on night sky

**MATERIALS:**
sponge cut into small pieces
acrylic paints
container of water
newspaper
tin cans from soup, coffee, or fruit

**PROCESS:**
1. Remove label from tin cans. Wash and dry cans.
2. Moisten sponges in water.
3. Squeeze acrylic paints onto newspaper.
4. Dip sponges into paints and dab onto cans.
5. Let dry.
6. Fill cans with pencils, crayons, or other treasured items, or use the decorated can as a gift container.

**VARIATIONS:**
**Cover cans with a rectangle of paper.**
**Then decorate paper with:**
1. sponge prints using tempera paint
2. finger prints and ink pads
3. crayon drawings
4. glued on scraps

# CARDBOARD BOX PAINTING

**MATERIALS:**
cardboard box
tempera paints
paint brushes
water
rags

**PROCESS:**
1. Paint box with tempera making a colorful scene, design or picture. Cover all sides.
2. Let dry.
2. Store books, toys, or favorite things in your painted box, or use as a small table or display case.

**VARIATIONS:**
1. Paint a variety of boxes and assemble as a box sculpture.
2. Paint a large appliance box to become a playhouse, rocketship, or hideout. Add doors, windows, and secret openings by carefully cutting cardboard.

CAUTION

**MATERIALS:**

water color or tempera paints
brush
water in container

plaster of Paris
pie tin or paper plate
stick for stirring

**PROCESS:**

Fresco means to paint with water based paint on wet plaster. The paint permeates the plaster and becomes a part of the plaster. Fresco means "fresh," referring to the wet plaster.

1. Mix plaster of Paris according to the box directions, and pour into a paper plate. Smooth with a stick. (Insert a hanging device such as a paper clip or loop of yarn if you wish.)

2. Paint on the wet plaster with tempera paints or water color paints. As long as the plaster is damp, fresco painting will be effective.

3. Allow plaster to dry.

4. Remove the plaster plaque from the paper plate.

5. Hang or use as a table or shelf decoration.

**VARIATIONS:**

1. Pour plaster in an identation in the sand at the beach for a plaster casting. Paint.

2. Pour plaster in a box. Tear away cardboard when dry.

3. Make a mold for the plaster in other ways, such as a ring of heavy paper in a base of Plasticine clay.

# IMPASTO

**MATERIALS:**
tempera paint
liquid starch
dark paper
drawing objects (paper clip, comb, stick, plastic fork)

**PROCESS:**
1. Mix tempera paint with liquid starch until thick and fluffy.
2. Brush a thick layer over dark paper.
3. Draw designs through paint.
4. Paint over the surface and begin again, if desired.

**VARIATIONS:**
1. Make a comb out of cardboard and draw through paint design.
2. Dip cardboard comb into multi-colors of paint and pull across paper. Make interesting, three-color designs.
3. Dip a popsicle stick into the paint and starch mixture, spreading it on paper in globs. Allow to dry. Add more layers and more colors, drying between layers. Resembles a true oil painting.

# PLASTIC SCRIMSHAW

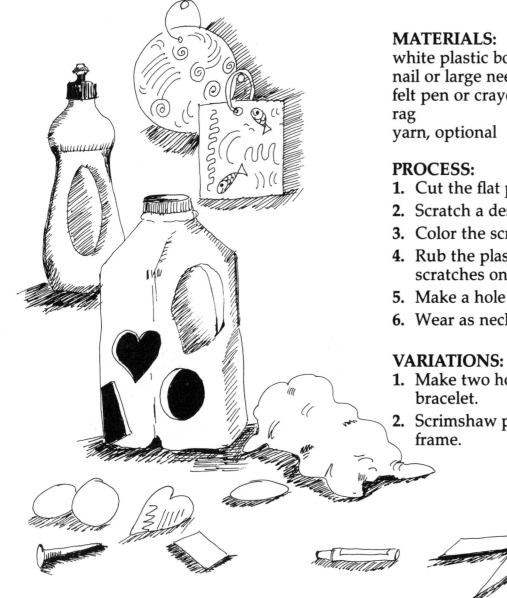

**MATERIALS:**
white plastic bottle
nail or large needle
felt pen or crayon
rag
yarn, optional

**PROCESS:**
1. Cut the flat part of a plastic bottle into a shape.
2. Scratch a design into the plastic with the needle or nail.
3. Color the scratches with pen or crayons.
4. Rub the plastic with the rag. Color will be left inside the scratches only.
5. Make a hole at the top of the scrimshaw design, if desired.
6. Wear as necklace or hang to view.

**VARIATIONS:**
1. Make two holes in the design, insert ribbon, and wear as bracelet.
2. Scrimshaw picture can be glued to a cardboard or other frame.

# PLASTIC PAINT BAGS

**MATERIALS:**
fingerpaint
plastic bag (used, clean, with no holes)
tape, optional
spoon

**PROCESS:**
1. Spoon colorful fingerpaint inside a large plastic bag.
2. Close tightly with tape, or use a ziploc variety.
3. Press designs with fingers into bag and watch paint move aside to make designs.

**VARIATIONS:**
1. Try other colored mixtures instead of paint:
   pudding
   mustard or ketchup
   lotion
2. Experiment with adding other little bits and fancies inside the paint, such as confetti, pieces of lace, or tiny shreads of fabric. Use nothing sharp that might poke a hole in the bag.

# SLATE SHINGLE PAINTINGS

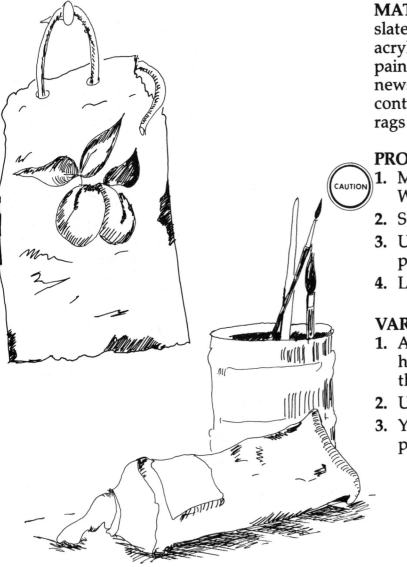

**MATERIALS:**
slate shingle
acrylic paints
paintbrushes
newspaper
container of water
rags

**PROCESS:**

1. Make sure shingle is clean and dry and free of insects. When handling beware of sharp edges.
2. Squeeze acrylic paints onto newspaper.
3. Use paintbrushes and paints to create a colorful design or picture on the slate.
4. Let dry.

**VARIATIONS:**

1. A simple hand drill (non-electric) can be used to drill a hole in the top of the slate. Thread heavy string or twine through the hole and hang.
2. Use a rock or piece of chalk to draw on slate.
3. Young children enjoy painting on slate with water and paintbrush.

# ROOFING FELT DRAWINGS

**MATERIALS:**
roofing felt (from local contractor, roofer, or lumber yard)
colored pencils (Prisma Color works well)
heavy scissors

**PROCESS:**
1. Cut a piece of roofing felt to a comfortable working size.
2. Lay it on a flat surface.
3. Draw a colorful scene, design or picture with colored pencils onto the felt.

**VARIATIONS:**
1. Paint a thin coat of gesso, latex paint, or white tempera paint on roofing felt to prime. Let dry. Draw on primed surface for a different effect.
2. Glue broken jewelry to roofing felt to enhance design.
3. Add any decorative items such as beans, seeds, macaroni, glitter, or feathers.

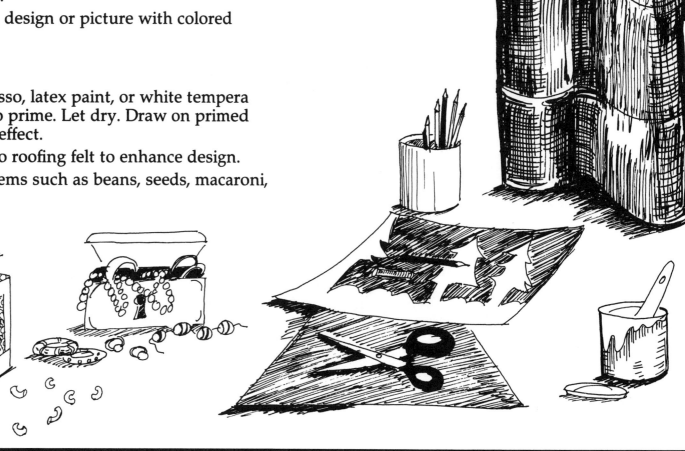

# NATURE RUBBINGS

**MATERIALS:**
newspaper
crayons (with paper peeled off)
fresh green leaves or wildflowers
paper

**PROCESS:**
1. Spread newspaper onto work surface.
2. Place leaves or wildflowers on the newspaper.
3. Place paper on top of leaves or wildflowers.
4. Hold a crayon sideways and rub over the leaves or wildflowers.
   (Hint: Feel them with your hands.)
5. Watch the leaves and wildflowers appear as you rub them over with crayons.

**VARIATIONS:**
1. Try making different patterns by arranging leaves and wildflowers in rows, circles.
2. Gather other things from nature, such as reeds, grasses, weeds.
3. Take your paper out into the world and make rubbings from surfaces such as tree bark, brick walls, and shingles.
4. Paint over crayon rubbing with thinned, watery paint for a crayon resist.

# STONE PAINTING

**MATERIALS:**
small, smooth stones
tempera paints
paintbrushes
newspaper to cover the table
a cup or jar of water
rags

**PROCESS:**
1. Wash and dry stones.
2. Paint designs and pictures on the stones.
3. Let dry.
4. Give as a gift or keep to enjoy.

**VARIATIONS:**
1. Glue rocks to a wood scrap or piece of cardboard. Decorate or paint in a pattern or design.
2. Color stones with crayon. Place in oven on low until crayon melts.
3. Put stones in garden to enjoy.

CAUTION

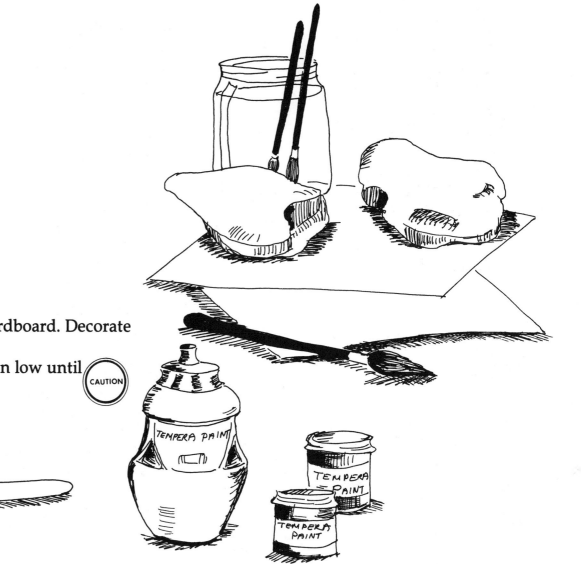

# INDOOR RAINBOW

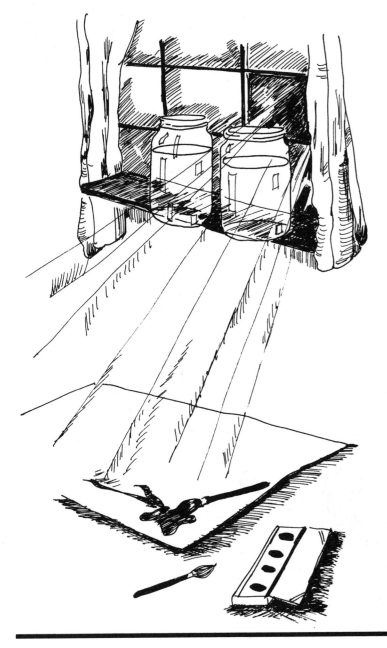

**MATERIALS:**
clear glass filled with water to the top
window sill
bright sunlight
white paper
water color paints or crayons

**PROCESS:**
1. Fill a glass with water to the top.
2. Set glass on window sill in bright sunlight.
3. Glass should stick out over the ledge a little bit.
4. Place a white piece of paper on the floor beneath the window.
5. Capture the rainbow on the paper.
6. Paint or color the paper to match the rainbow.
7. Remove the paper and enjoy the artistic rainbow.

**VARIATIONS:**
1. Create a rainbow outside with a garden hose. The sun must be shining, with your back to the sun. Make a fine mist with the hose and find the rainbow.
2. Using colored tissue, make rainbows by sticking tissue to white paper with liquid starch or thinned white glue.

# SHADOW DRAWING

**MATERIALS:**
large piece of paper
pens
sunlight and shadow

**PROCESS:**
1. Find a shadow you like.
2. Place paper on ground so that shadow is on paper.
3. Draw around the outline of the shadow.
4. Your drawing is complete.

**VARIATIONS:**
1. Paint or color in some of the spaces or designs outlined in pen.
2. Use same paper to add more shadows, overlapping lines if desired.
3. Make a theme drawing such as "Objects on the Playground", "My Favorite Friends", "Flowers of Spring", and so on.
4. Have someone trace your own shadow. Then paint or color the drawing to be you or an imaginary form of you.
5. Trace a shadow on the sidewalk with chalk.

# COTTON BALL CLOUDS

**MATERIALS:**
cotton balls
white glue
pencil
paper
crayons
sand, grass, pine needles, leaves, bark (optional)

**PROCESS:**
1. Observe the clouds in the sky.
2. Draw cloud shapes onto paper.
3. Glue cotton balls onto the cloud shapes, pulling cotton into thin and wispy shapes or into fluffy and thick shapes.
4. Let dry.
5. Use crayons to add to your creations, if desired.

**VARIATIONS:**
1. Try making a grassy field by observing a field and using grasses.
2. Try making a sandy beach using sand.
3. Try making the "woods" by using pieces of dry bark, pine needles, and leaves from trees.
4. Use cotton balls to create a snow, fog, or cotton candy design.

# SAND PAINTINGS

**MATERIALS:**
dry sand (in paper cups or small containers)
white glue
paper or cardboard
newspaper
pencil
crayons

**PROCESS:**
1. Use pencil to draw a design or picture lightly on the paper.
2. Apply a bead of glue to the pencil lines.
3. Sprinkle sand gently over wet glue.
4. Tilt the paper up so that the extra sand falls off the paper onto an open sheet of newspaper.
5. Let dry.
6. Use crayons to add other details or color to the sand painting.

**VARIATIONS:**
1. Try making a free flowing design without using the pencil first. Squeeze glue onto the paper quickly and see what you can create!
2. Try brushing glue from a cup here and there over paper. Add sand to glue. Shake off excess.

# POTS, PANS, AND PAPER

**MATERIALS:**
pots, pans
newspaper or other throwaway paper
paper grocery bags
paste or white glue
pencil
crayons, markers, or colored pencils
scissors

**PROCESS:**
1. Cut grocery bag into a squarish-flat shape.
2. Put aside.
3. Open newspaper and trace the bottom side of pots and pans.
4. Cut out the shapes with scissors.
5. Paste shapes on grocery bag.
6. Decorate with crayons, pencils or markers, if desired.

**VARIATIONS:**
1. Use other household items to trace such as spatulas, lids, hammers, hair brushes, shoes, or hands and feet.
2. Try pasting shapes on the bag without cutting it up for a creative carrying tote!
3. Go outdoors and trace objects.
4. Paint shapes instead of cutting them out.

# JUNKYARD PAINTINGS

## MATERIALS:
paper or cardboard
spray paint
collected junk such as cans, old combs, old tools, chains

## PROCESS:
1. Arrange junk on paper or cardboard.
2. Spray junk lightly with paint.
3. Rearrange junk.
   (Hint: You will be able to see an impression of your items on the paper.)
4. Spray lightly again.
5. Continue to rearrange and spray junk to make a creative junkyard design.
6. Let dry.

## VARIATIONS:
Try —
1. Glue junk to cardboard. Dry. Spray with silver paint for a gilded relief design.
2. Glue junk to cardboard. Dry. Cover with used aluminum foil until entire relief is covered.

# SNOW PAINTINGS

**MATERIALS:**
spray bottles and liquid soap bottles
food coloring, water, or watered down tempera paint
snow

**PROCESS:**
1. Fill bottles with colored water.
2. Find a fresh area of snow to create paintings.
3. Spray the area of snow with your bottles of colored water.

**VARIATIONS:**
1. Create designs, pictures, or scenes on the snow.
2. Fill a pan with snow and spray color designs in the pan.

# ICE-Y ART

**MATERIALS:**
butcher paper
powdered tempera paint in salt shaker
ice cubes or icicles
mittens

**PROCESS:**
1. Lay butcher paper on floor or outside.
2. Put on mittens.
3. Sprinkle several colors of powdered tempera on the paper.
4. Hold an ice cube or icicle and draw it through the paint.

**VARIATIONS:**
Try —
1. Add bits of white confetti to the paint when finished drawing.
2. Shake salt from a salt shaker on the paint and watch the magic.

# POSTER TIME

**MATERIALS:**
large poster paper (ask a print shop for left-over paper)
paints, pens, crayons
paper scraps
glue

**PROCESS:**
1. Decide on a topic you want to highlight in the poster. (Examples: a favorite book, how to protect the earth, advertise something you like)
2. Start painting, drawing, and/or gluing as you design and create the poster.
3. Dry.
4. Display at home or find someone who might like to have the poster in their store, office, or school.

**VARIATIONS:**
1. Look at posters for sale in the store and get ideas of artwork to use for your poster.
2. Cut used posters and use parts you like to make a collage poster with a new idea.
3. Make a poster that shows you care about something (like protecting endangered animals) and have it displayed somewhere it will help the cause (like at the library or zoo).

# MY OWN BOOK

**MATERIALS:**

old sheet or cotton table cloth
used shoe laces, yarn, or embroidery thread
permanent laundry marker
sewing machine or threaded needle

scissors
fabric pens
sewing pins

**PROCESS:**

1. Cut or tear sheet into rectangles (which will be the size of the book).

2. Stack rectangles, matching corners. (These are the pages.)

3. Fold material in half, and mark with pins.

4. Hand sew or machine sew up the center of the rectangles to hold all firmly together.

5. Draw on scraps of fabric with fabric pens.

6. Attach shoe lace or yarn to each drawing by hand sewing.

7. Cut two tiny slits in page and tie drawing to slits.

8. Cut as many spots for tying as desired on each page.

9. Write captions with laundry pen to describe each drawing.

**VARIATIONS:**

1. Move drawings around from page to page for changing the story line.

2. Cover paper drawings with clear contact paper, punch a hole in the top, and substitute for fabric drawings.

3. Book can be an original story, a scrap book of different thoughts and likes, or a re-telling of a favorite story.

   Lots of options here!

# SHEET BANNERS

**MATERIALS:**
old sheet or pillow case
scissors
coat hanger
tempera paints
paint brushes
cup of water
rags
stapler

**PROCESS:**
1. Cut sheet or pillow case to fit the width of the coat hanger. Make it as long as you like.
2. Paint a colorful scene, picture or design onto the cloth.
3. Let dry.
4. Bend top of banner over the bottom of the coat hanger and staple into place.
5. Hang to display.

**VARIATIONS:**
1. Make the banner from any paper, joining many sheets of paper with glue to form a long banner.
2. Use fabric crayons to decorate old sheets for a permanent, washable banner.
3. Use printing techniques such as vegetable prints to make design.
4. Use fabric pens for design.

# WALL HANGING

**MATERIALS:**
fabric scrap
two sticks, such as broken broom handles or large twigs
paint, such as tempera or acrylic
yarn threaded on darning needle
string, longer than one stick
two tacks

**PROCESS:**
1. Cut or trim fabric scrap to desired shape. Iron if necessary.
2. Place fabric right side down on table.
3. Place stick at top and fold fabric over stick. Straight stitch through both pieces.
   (Hint: Fabric may be glued or stapled to stick at this point instead of sewn, if desired.)
4. Repeat at bottom of fabric.
5. Turn fabric over.
6. Paint on fabric.
7. Attach string to each end of stick at top for hanging with tacks. Staples, glue, or tying also works well.
8. Use for hanging on wall, as a screen between rooms, or over a window.

**VARIATIONS:**
1. Instead of paint, use fabric crayons, fabric dye, or fabric pens.
2. Omit sticks and make a table decoration, pillow, or framed fabric painting.

# GLUE BATIK

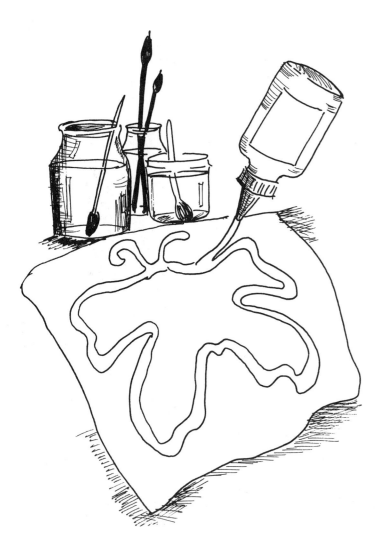

## MATERIALS:
white cotton fabric (old sheet, T-shirt)
several containers to mix colors
poster, tag, or illustration board (optional)
stapler (optional)

white glue
tempera paints
water
paintbrushes

## PROCESS:
1. Place cotton or muslin on a flat surface.
2. Create a design or picture on cotton or muslin with glue. Dry.
3. Paint with lightest colors (yellow, pink, orange) over the design. Dry.
4. Repeat step #2, drawing with glue. Dry.
5. Paint with darker colors (red, violet, blue, green) over the design. Dry.
6. Staple batik on poster board for display, if desired.
7. *Do not wash.*

## VARIATIONS:
1. Try making a single color batik.
2. Sew your batik into a pillow by stitching another piece of cotton or muslin onto the back. Leave one side open and stuff with fabric scraps, fiberfill, or cattail fluff. Stitch to close.
3. Stretch batik over cardboard and tape on back with masking tape. Possibly stuff between cardboard and batik for a "puff design".
4. Mat and frame batik.

# T-SHIRT TRANSFERS

**MATERIALS:**
fabric crayons, available in craft or fabric stores
used poly/cotton T-shirt                    iron
white drawing paper                         scissors (optional)

**PROCESS:**
1. Follow directions on fabric crayon box.
2. Draw on white paper.
3. Place drawing face down on old T-shirt.
4. Move iron firmly over design on medium temperature setting.
5. Be careful not to move drawing, or a double image will result.
6. Remove drawing.
7. Drawing has transferred to the T-shirt.
8. Add additional designs to shirt as desired, repeating steps 2 through 6.
   (Hint: Fabric crayon transfers are washable, machine dryable, and wonderfully permanent.)

**VARIATIONS:**

**Recycle old fabric items such as:**
1. sheets or pillow cases
2. handkerchiefs
3. aprons

**Try — making an old sheet into:**
1. pillow coverings
2. baby quilt
3. wall hanging
4. book bag
5. doll blanket

**NOTE:**
Very young children need adult supervision or help with ironing.

# DRAW FROM NATURE

**MATERIALS:**
charcoal sticks or pencils
paper
eraser (optional)
book or board to hold paper on your lap
paints and brushes, water and rags (optional)

**PROCESS:**
1. Find a place or scene that you think is interesting to draw. It could be a sunny field, a quiet path in the woods, a sandy beach, or a dry desert. Or look out the window at the scenery.
2. Sit in a comfortable position and place your board on your lap.
3. Observe what is around you.
4. Draw what you see.

**VARIATIONS:**
1. Use paints instead of pencils or charcoal to paint a colorful scene.
2. Try using your imagination to draw or paint the sound of the ocean, the wind, a creek, the song of a bird, or the sounds of animals.
3. Close your eyes and draw, never lifting your pencil from the paper.
4. Draw on: shells, brick, sidewalk, wood, rocks, driveway.

**HOW TO MAKE CHARCOAL STICKS:**
Charcoal is what remains of a campfire after it has been put out and is cold. Use a burned, blackened twig or stick as a drawing stick.

# BRACKET FUNGI PAINTING

## MATERIALS:
paints
jar of water
paintbrushes
paper towels or rags
newspaper
bracket fungi
pencil

## PROCESS:
1. Gather some bracket fungi, which grows on the sides of trees in wooded areas.
   (Hint: Make sure that the fungi is dry and free of dirt before starting your painting.)
2. Spread newspaper over a flat surface and place fungi on it.
   (Hint: You can sketch a design or picture on the fungi with a pencil before painting it.)
3. Paint your bracket fungi with your paints in a colorful and creative way.
4. Let dry.

## VARIATIONS:
1. Use painted fungi as a bookend, paperweight or shelf decoration.
2. Carve or scratch design into fungi with nail, paperclip, or other sharp object. Paint or leave as is.

**MATERIALS:**
leaf
paper
sponge piece
inked stamp pad

**PROCESS:**
1. Hold a leaf on a sheet of paper with one hand.
2. Ink a piece of soft sponge on an ink pad.
3. Brush the sponge outward from the leaf edge onto the paper.
4. Remove the leaf.
5. Repeat as often as you like.

**VARIATIONS:**
1. Use many colors of ink pads for a rainbow effect.
2. Move leaf silhouettes down a long piece of paper to become a banner.
3. Repeat this project on a white cardboard gift box as the wrapping design.
4. Make wrapping paper by using a thin white paper.
5. Make note cards by folding a heavy paper and then printing on the front.
6. Trace a leaf on a file folder or tag board. Cut out the leaf shape. Draw *inside* the cut-out with chalk. Before moving cut-out, rub with a tissue for a solid leaf design. Then remove.

# LEAF BURSTS

**MATERIALS:**

newspaper

paper

paint brushes

tempera paints

container with water

paintbrushes

rags

fresh green leaves

**PROCESS:**
1. Cover table with newspaper.
2. Place paper on newspaper.
3. Put leaf on paper.
   (Hint: Hold the leaf still with one hand and use the other hand to paint on the leaf, brushing in an outward direction.)
4. Move leaf to another part of the paper and repeat painting.
5. Use another leaf to create more leaf burst designs.

**VARIATIONS:**
1. Staple painted leaves to your finished leaf burst design.
2. Use cut shapes and patterns from tag board or old file folders and create "pattern bursts".
3. Try using chalk instead of paint. Rub or brush chalk marks with tissue.

# FILM ETCHING

**MATERIALS:**
blank movie film, choose 16mm or 8mm
  (Ask a TV station or movie processing store for the white or black leader tape that preceeds the movie. Lots of films are being discarded since the onset of video movies, so they are easy to get.)
nail or large needle
felt pens (permanent colors work best)
newspaper
tape
movie projector with reels (same size as film being etched, either 16mm or 8mm)

**PROCESS:**
1. Cover table or floor with newspaper.
2. Unwind blank black or white leader film from film reel.
3. Tape each end of the film to the newspaper.
4. Using a nail or large needle, scratch designs into the black or white film. Be careful not to poke holes in the film. (Note: Repeating tiny designs will give an animated effect. Larger, unplanned designs will give a flashing, random effect.)
5. Next, color the scratches with permanent colored felt pens in any way desired.
6. Rewind the scratched or etched, colored film back onto the reel. Tape several shorter film segments together to increase the length of the film.
7. After an adult sets up the projector, watch the etched film.
8. After watching, make more films, experimenting with animation, repetition, and design.

**VARIATIONS:**
1. Add music to the film from a tape or CD.
2. Tape a commentary for the film, telling a story or describing the action on the screen.

# SCULPTURE AND MOBILES

chapter 2

# HANGING BOX ART

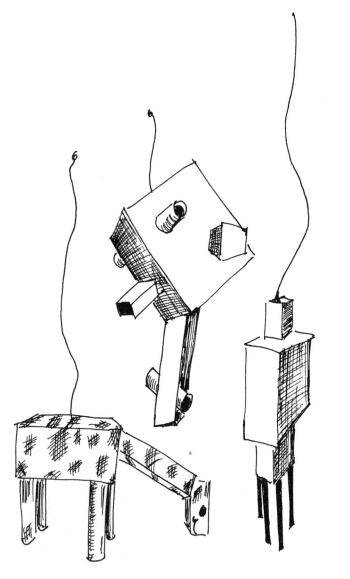

**MATERIALS:**

cardboard boxes, all shapes and sizes
cardboard tubes
tempera paint or wrapping paper
tape
white glue
heavy yarn or string
collage materials (optional)

**PROCESS:**
1. Decide if sculpture will be painted or decorated with wrapping paper.
2. If using wrapping paper, wrap all boxes with scraps of wrapping paper before beginning sculpture. If painting, do this later.
3. Tape boxes and tubes together in any abstract designs. Make as many separate sculptures as desired.
4. If painting sculpture, do this now. Dry.
5. String sculptures together with yarn or string, joining several small sculptures if desired.
6. Hang from ceiling or light fixture.

**VARIATIONS:**
1. Instead of painting or covering boxes with wrapping, spray paint all boxes with clear enamel.
2. Cover boxes with magazine pictures trying for themes such as happy faces, favorite foods, things to wish for, and so on.
3. Add other decorative items such as ribbons, stickers, shells, or small toys.

# STRING SWAG

**MATERIALS:**

cupcake liners
scraps of paper
drinking straws
styrofoam peanuts
macaroni
yarn or string
plastic darning needle

**PROCESS:**
1. Thread needle with yarn and knot both loose ends together.
2. Begin stringing scraps, straws, and papers in any random or planned order. Use creativity in collecting your supplies. Anything you can push the needle through will work.
3. When yarn is full, cut and tie end.
4. Thread a new needle with yarn and tie to old yarn to continue stringing.
5. Continue until swag is desired length.
6. Hang swag in draped designs anywhere desired, such as around windows, across mantlepiece, or along ceiling edge.

**VARIATIONS:**
1. Hang swag as a party decoration.
2. Add ribbons, foil, dyed coffee filters, pieces of greeting cards, and other pretty bits of this and that.
3. Make a small swag and wear as a necklace or Hawaiian lei.
4. Wrap round and round a post or column for a May-pole effect.

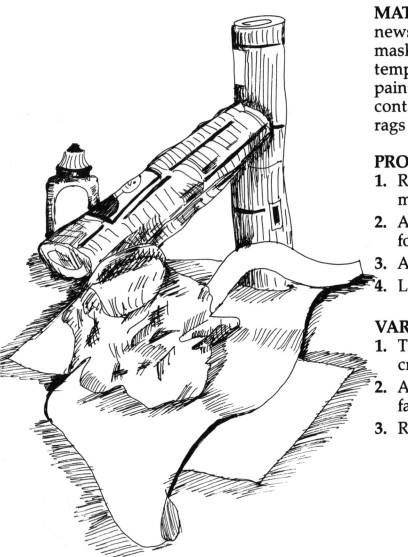

**MATERIALS:**
newspaper
masking tape
tempera paints
paintbrushes
container of water
rags

**PROCESS:**
1. Roll or crush newspaper into any shapes and wrap with masking tape.
2. Attach different shapes together with masking tape to form an interesting sculpture.
3. Add color with tempera paints, if desired.
4. Let dry.

**VARIATIONS:**
1. Try making an octopus, dog, snake, dragon, or other creature.
2. Add decorative items such as broken jewelry, yarn, doilies, fabric, or buttons.
3. Roll newspaper around a dowel for a strong tube.

# PAPER TUBE SCULPTURE

**MATERIALS:**
paper tube (toilet paper, paper towel or wrapping paper tubes)
piece of cardboard for a base (pizza box works well)
white glue
tempera paint
scissors
paintbrush
water
rags
newspaper (to cover work surface)

**PROCESS:**
1. Cut paper tubes into a variety of shapes and sizes.
2. Glue paper tubes to the cardboard base.
3. Let dry.
4. Paint your sculpture with tempera paint, if desired.
5. Let dry.
6. Display your sculpture on a shelf or in a favorite place.

**VARIATION:**
Add other recycled items for decorations such as:

| | |
|---|---|
| jar lids | scraps of paper |
| yarn | packing peanuts |
| feathers | beads |
| macaroni | |

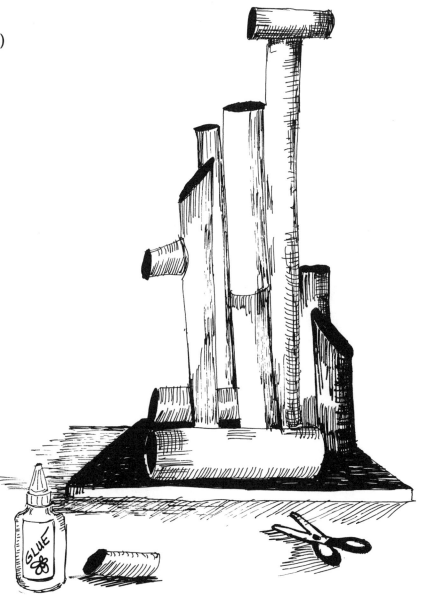

# SHADOW ART

**MATERIALS:**
lightweight cardboard from department store clothing boxes, food boxes (cereal, donuts), tag, or poster board
heavy cardboard from boxes
scissors
white glue

**PROCESS:**
1. Cut lightweight cardboard into strips.
2. Cut a square piece of cardboard from the heavy cardboard box to form a background.
3. Glue strips of the lightweight cardboard on edge to the background.
4. Create interesting shapes and designs by cutting the cardboard strips in various lengths and glue into place.
5. Let dry.
6. Place your shadow art creation near a strong source of light and watch the shadows that are created!

**VARIATIONS:**
1. Add sand, crushed egg shells, beans, or grains to the separate sections for a texture or collage effect.
2. Cover the background with thin paper or paint a bright color before adding strips of lightweight cardboard.
3. Instead of a flat board as a background, try making your shadow art on the inside of a shoe box. Stack several boxes together for a larger, mixed display.

# MAT BOARD SCULPTURE

**MATERIALS:**
mat board pieces
heavy scissors
white glue or craft glue

**PROCESS:**
1. Gather pieces of mat board in several sizes, shapes and colors.
2. Put a larger mat board piece down to form a base.
3. Glue little pieces and strips of mat board on top to form sculpture or design.

**VARIATIONS:**
1. Cut small, thin strips of thin cardboard — such as tag board or lightweight cardboard from clothing boxes — and glue together in a squiggle or loop design.
2. For a group project, assemble several mat board sculptures together as one large sculpture.

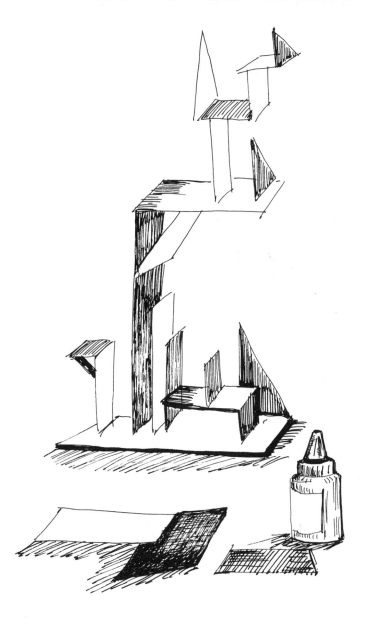

# CARDBOARD CITY

**MATERIALS:**
cardboard cut into assorted rectangles, triangles, squares
large cardboard rectangle or square
heavy scissors
white glue
tempera paints
paintbrushes, water, and rags

**PROCESS:**
1. Place large piece of cardboard on a flat surface.
2. Glue smaller pieces of cardboard on top of large piece to form skyscrapers, houses, and towers. Overlap buildings, and place smaller buildings on top of larger ones.
3. Let dry.
4. Paint cardboard city in a colorful way.
5. Let dry and display.

**VARIATIONS:**
1. Try making an ocean scene, a country scene, or enjoy the shapes in any design.
2. Paint your city background dark blue and buildings black and grey for a night scene. Add glitter stars and a foil moon.

# CEREAL BOX BUILDINGS

**MATERIALS:**
cereal boxes or light weight boxes (tissue, cracker, or cookie boxes)
scissors
white glue
tempera paints or acrylic paints
paintbrushes
container of water and rags
brushes
pencil

**PROCESS:**
1. Draw rectangles, squares and other shapes onto cardboard boxes to represent windows and doors.
2. Cut out shapes with scissors.
3. Glue additional pieces of cardboard onto box to form roofs, flower boxes, trellis, steps, railings.
4. Let dry.
5. Paint.
6. Let dry.

**VARIATIONS:**
1. Try making people from cardboard to live in your buildings.
2. Try making cars, horses, trees, and ponds.
3. Join many buildings on a large sheet of cardboard to make a city or town. Add sidewalks, roads, parks, and playgrounds.

# PAPER TRASH SCULPTURE

**MATERIALS:**

junk mail
magazines and newspapers
wrapping paper
tissue rolls

egg cartons
pizza boxes
other paper trash
stapler, tape, or glue

**PROCESS:**

1. Collect junk and trash made from paper.
2. Assemble pieces into a sculpture, using stapler, tape, and/or glue.
   Note: Glue guns work well for older children, but should be carefully supervised due to danger from hot tip of gun.
3. Attach sculpture to a cardboard base such as a pizza box or lid from a box, if desired.
4. Title the sculpture like professional artists do.

**VARIATION:**

Try adding metal, plastic, or other trash to sculpture.
Choose items such as:
  six-pack rings
  margarine tubs
  yogurt containers
  bottle caps
  plastic forks
  plastic bags
  juice cans

# ACES WILD SCULPTURE

**MATERIALS:**
old deck of playing cards
scissors

**PROCESS:**
1. Cut two slits on each side of each card. Slits could be about ½ inch long.
2. Begin sliding cards together, fitting one slit into another slit.
3. Continue until desired sculpture is achieved.
4. Take apart and start again for a new design.

**VARIATIONS:**
1. Before making slits, cover cards with newspaper, pretty scrap paper, stickers, or rectangles cut from posters.
2. Try using the cards to build, but join them with 2″ pieces of drinking straws with a slit cut into each end. The straws become the connectors for the card structure.
3. Glue playing cards into a collage, use for a mobile, or cut into bitty pieces for a mosaic.

# PAPER BAG SCULPTURE

**MATERIALS:**
paper bags, any sizes
string, twine, or tape
scissors
tempera paints
newspaper
paintbrushes
water in jar
rags

**PROCESS:**
1. Stuff paper bag full with crumpled newspaper. Tie or tape securely at the top.
2. Paint a design, scene or picture onto the bag.
3. Let dry and display.

**VARIATIONS:**
1. Paint a Jack-O-Lantern.
2. Try stuffing some paper in the bottom of the bag and tie string in the middle. Stuff more paper and re-tie for a sculpture effect.
3. Tie several bag sculptures in a row as a ceiling decoration or garland.
4. Use unpainted bags as sculpture blocks, building and taping them together.

# STUFFED BROWN BAG

**MATERIALS:**

paper grocery bag
scissors
pencil
newspaper or scrap paper
stapler and staples

tempera paints, crayons, or markers
paintbrush
water
rags
string

**PROCESS:**
1. Cut open paper bag so that there are two brown sheets of paper which are about the same size.
2. Draw the outline of any shape on one piece of paper and cut it out.
3. Use this as a pattern and trace around it on the other piece of paper.
4. Staple both pieces of paper together along the outside edges, leaving one end opened for stuffing.
5. Color or paint both sides of the shape and let dry.
6. Tear newspaper or scrap paper into small pieces and stuff into the shape. (Crumple newspaper for faster stuffing.)
7. Staple closed.
8. Poke a hole into the shape and tie on a string.
9. Hang up for display.

**VARIATIONS:**
1. Try making a fish, bird, monster, or dinosaur.
2. Use as a gift bag and fill design with homemade treasures or gifts.
3. Make a school of fish.
4. Make a family of creatures.
5. Paper can be sewn on sewing machine instead of stapled.

# DOLL'S PLAY HOUSE

**MATERIALS:**
box with large base
patterned paper (wallpaper scraps are good)
carpet scraps or fabric scraps
glue
scissors
knife

**PROCESS:**
1. Cut away one long side of the box, and one short side next to it. You have an L-shaped wall.
2. Cover the walls with patterned paper.
3. Cover the floor with carpet or fabric.
4. Make furniture out of cut-away box scraps. Decorate.

**VARIATIONS:**
1. Divide one room into two or four sections and decorate each one as a room in the house.
2. Instead of a house, decorate the box to be a garden, a space ship, a school, an office, a hospital, or whatever you like.
3. Use anything you can think of to add to the house or scene: marbles, beads, bottle caps, match boxes, small framed pictures, shells, straws, doilies, and more. If you can't find what you need, make it yourself.

# SHADOW BOX

## MATERIALS:
shoe box
scissors
rubber cement, glue, tape or stapler
any paints or coloring tools
scrap papers
scrap materials:

| | | | | |
|---|---|---|---|---|
| felt | yarn | clay | wire | sand |
| ribbon | buttons | pipe cleaners | pebbles | etc. |

## PROCESS:
1. Decide on a scene, story, or design.
2. Design the background first.
3. Make trees, houses, figures, grass, and other props as desired. Use imagination as to what materials are necessary.
4. Allow to dry.

## VARIATIONS:
1. Possibilities are unlimited as are scrap materials. Have fun!
2. Make several shadow boxes which work together to form a story, scene, or experiment in color and design.

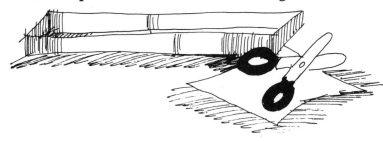

# WIRE FIGURES

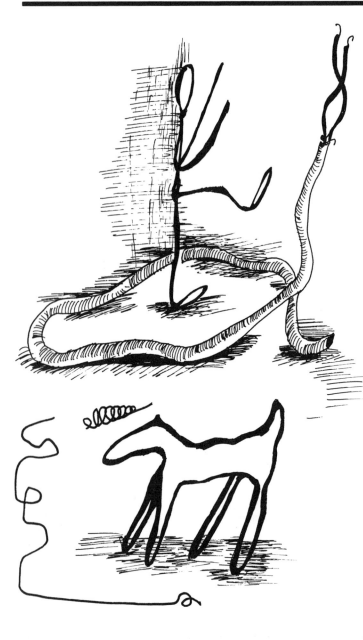

**MATERIALS:**
flexible wire (scraps from telephone company are perfect)
scissors or cutting tool

**PROCESS:**
1. Bend and twist wires into desired shapes.
2. Experiment with coils wrapped around sticks, pencils, bottles, and fingers.
   Note: Make sure coils can be removed.
3. Wire figures may be one continuous piece of wire, or many pieces joined together.
4. When complete, try bending figures into different postures. Figures will be free-standing.

**VARIATIONS:**
1. Add other materials to figures such as sponges, plastics, wood, and fabric.
2. Figures may be mounted on a block of used packing styrofoam or attached to nails in a block of wood.

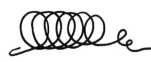

# MACHINE SCULPTURE

**MATERIALS:**
car parts
bits of other broken machines
wire or heavy tape
model glue

**PROCESS:**
1. Collect car parts from an auto-recycling yard. Look for a variety of interesting shapes.
2. Collect parts of any broken machines, such as calculators, alarm clocks, old radios, televisions, and more.
3. Begin assembling parts and pieces in a design of your choice. Use heavy tape and wire to attach pieces to each other, or use model glue. (Supervision required for glue.)
4. Build until satisfied with work.
5. Consider naming the work of art.

**VARIATIONS:**
1. Prepare a flat design by nailing, gluing, and attaching parts and pieces to a piece of wood or cardboard. Paint, if desired.
2. Build a silly or fantasy clock from a broken clock. Add other parts and decorations.
3. Build an imaginary machine from parts and pieces.

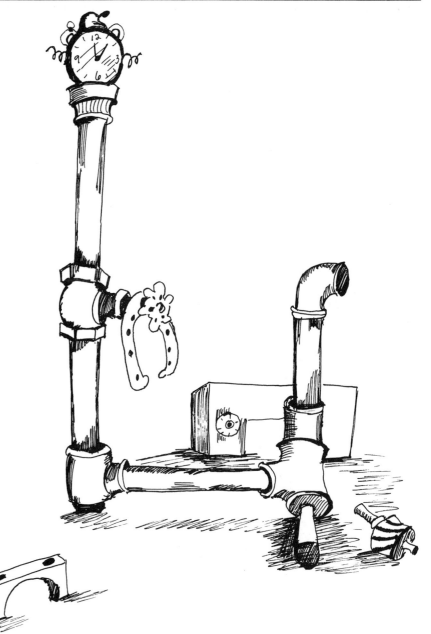

# DESIGN JARS

**MATERIALS:**
baby food jar and lid (or any jar with tight fitting lid)
pencil
colored paper
glue
scissors

**PROCESS:**
1. Trace around the jar opening on colored paper.
2. Cut out the circle.
3. Make a little stand-up design with paper, and glue it to the circle.
4. With the lid as a base, push the design into the lid.
5. Screw the jar over the design in the lid.
6. Display design with the lid as the base.

**VARIATIONS:**
1. Glue a dried flower to the circle and display in the jar.
2. Glue any special collected item such as a shell, stone, or pinecone into the jar.
3. To display a shell (or stone), glue the shell to the inside of the lid. Then fill the jar with salad oil, add glitter for snow if desired, and screw on lid. The color of the shell will be heightened by the oil.

# SOAP CARVINGS

**MATERIALS:**
cake of soap
butter knife
potato peeler

**PROCESS:**
1. Use a potato peeler to carve and shape a design into the soap.
2. Use a butter knife to cut off large areas.
3. Shape and carve soap into desired design.
4. Display your carving, or use in the tub or sink.

**VARIATIONS:**
1. Try drawing a scene into the surface of the soap with a nail or toothpick.
2. Moisten several soap carvings and stick together as one carving.
3. Squeeze moistened carving scraps together to form soap balls.

# BREEZY RINGS

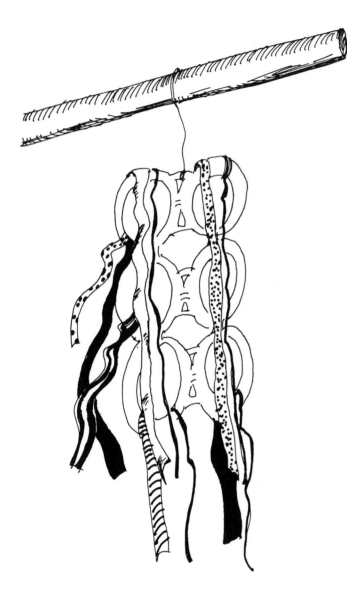

**MATERIALS:**
fabric or paper
six-pack rings (or coffee can lid with center cut out)
string, yarn
feathers
buttons
other odds and ends

**PROCESS:**
1. Hang the rings from a tree, fence, or swing set with string.
2. Slip-knot streamers of yarn, fabric, or paper through rings.
3. Add other items you would enjoy seeing blow in the wind.
4. Watch.
5. Be sure to bring rings indoors when done so animals will not pick them up.

**VARIATIONS:**
1. Find a stick and attach fabric and paper to top of stick to make a wand to blow in the wind.
2. Make a huge wind sculpture with noisy items to hang and blow in the wind, such as:
   blocks of wood
   plastic pipes
   cans and bottles

# STYROFOAM MOBILE

**MATERIALS:**
styrofoam meat trays
scissors
hole puncher
string
coat hanger
permanent markers or ball point pen (optional)
pencil

**PROCESS:**
1. Use a pencil to draw shapes into styrofoam meat trays.
2. Cut out shapes with scissors.
3. Punch hole in the top of shapes with a hole puncher.
4. Add additional details with permanent markers or ball point pens, if desired.
5. Place a string through each hole and attach to coat hanger.

**VARIATIONS:**
1. Glue collage items to styrofoam shapes. Let dry, then string for mobile.
2. Glue magazine pictures, wallpaper scraps, or gift wrap to shapes. Let dry. Then string for mobile.

# WIRE COAT HANGER MOBILE

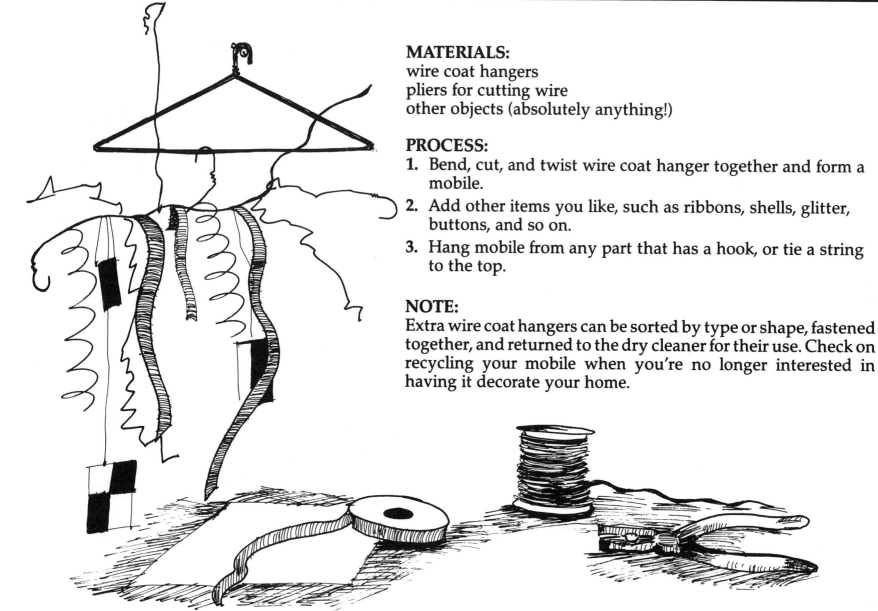

**MATERIALS:**
wire coat hangers
pliers for cutting wire
other objects (absolutely anything!)

**PROCESS:**
1. Bend, cut, and twist wire coat hanger together and form a mobile.
2. Add other items you like, such as ribbons, shells, glitter, buttons, and so on.
3. Hang mobile from any part that has a hook, or tie a string to the top.

**NOTE:**
Extra wire coat hangers can be sorted by type or shape, fastened together, and returned to the dry cleaner for their use. Check on recycling your mobile when you're no longer interested in having it decorate your home.

# HOOP MOBILE

## MATERIALS:
photographs
magazine pictures
file folders
glue
string
paper clips
tape
old hula hoop (or plastic pipe bent in a circle and taped)

## PROCESS:
1. Collect photographs of kids doing things during each season, or cut magazine pictures of the same theme.
2. Glue magazine pictures to old file folders cut in squares (or some other heavy paper).
3. Attach pictures to a hula hoop with string and paper clips ordering them in sequence, if desired.
   Note: paper clips are nice because you can change this mobile to other theme ideas by simply removing pictures from clips.
4. Hang at eye level so easily viewed.

## VARIATIONS:
1. Make a hoop mobile of a theme such as "What Makes Me Happy", "Favorite Pets", "Colors I Love", and so on.
2. Make a book of any of the above instead of a mobile. Add captions the child dictates.
3. Add captions the child dictates to the mobile.

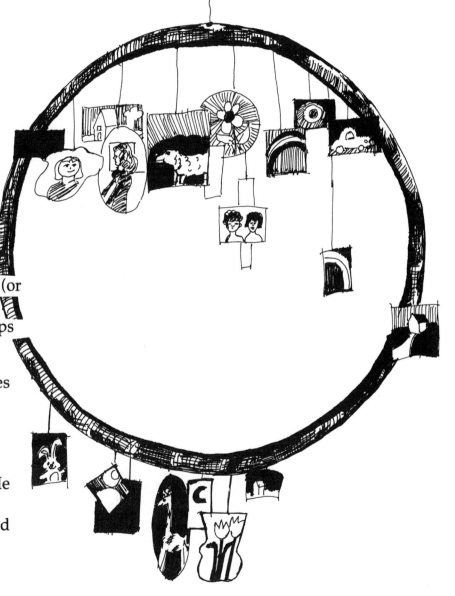

# CUP SCULPTURE

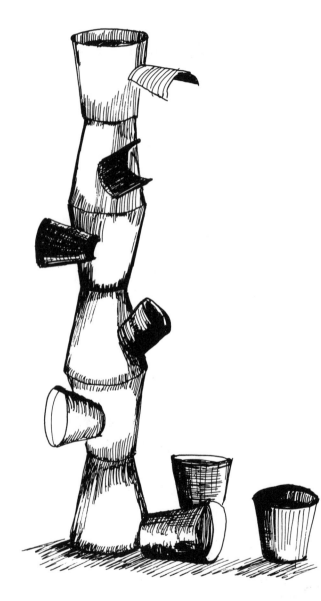

**MATERIALS:**
used, clean paper cups
tape
cardboard base or box lid
container filled with 1" of glue
paper tubes, optional
paints, optional

**PROCESS:**
1. Dip cups in glue and stick to other cups.
2. Add paper tubes or other paper items, if desired.
3. Continue building and sculpting.
4. Use tape so project can move along. Glue can take a long time to try.
5. When sculpture is dry, paint or decorate further, if desired.

**VARIATIONS:**
1. Cut tubes and cups into other shapes to use in sculpture.
2. Older children may use a glue gun for a rapid and strong sculpture, but adult supervision is suggested.
3. Try paper-clipping cups together. Take apart and assemble many times in a wide variety of designs.
4. Poke holes in cups and lace together with yarn or string.

# LID MOBILE

**MATERIALS:**
plastic lids from margarine containers, yogurt, or other lids
scissors
pencil
crayons or markers
hole punch
string
coat hanger
white craft glue such as Tacky glue or Sobo glue
paper

**PROCESS:**
1. Trace lid with pencil on any paper you like.
2. Cut out circles and glue onto each side of lid.
3. Make a hole in the top with a hole punch.
4. Decorate in a colorful way with crayons or markers.
5. Place string through each hole and tie to coat hanger.
6. Hang your mobile from the hook of the coat hanger.

**VARIATIONS:**
1. Cut designs from magazines, photographs, wrapping paper, or greeting cards and glue to lids.
2. Trace two photographs with a mayonnaise jar lid. Cut out. Glue photograph circles to each side of lid. Tie yarn around rim of lid, and hang.

# CAN SCULPTURE

**MATERIALS:**
cans from soup, coffee, vegetables
craft glue
masking or duct tape
clip clothes pins
scissors
can opener

**Optional Materials:**
spray paints
acrylic paints
sponges or brushes
newspaper or
    construction paper
dried flowers

**PROCESS:**
1. Open both ends of the cans with a can opener. Tape over sharp edges with masking tape or duct tape.
2. Peel off any labels on the cans and make sure that they are clean and dry before using.
3. Stack cans in an interesting way and glue together wherever they touch. Use clothes pins to hold into place until glue dries.
4. Remove clothes pins and thread tape through the inside and outside of cans wherever glue joints are to reinforce sculpture.

**VARIATIONS:**
1. Add color with acrylic paints using a sponge or brush.
2. Use spray paints to color the insides of the cans, and then spray the outsides of the cans in a contrasting color.
3. Cover cans first with scrap wrapping paper, newspaper or old posters.
4. Fill cans with fun or unusual decorative materials such as dried flowers, folded papers, or wires.
5. Make a magazine holder or towel rack.

# TIN CAN MOBILE

## MATERIALS:
tin cans from soup, canned milk, fruit, coffee
can opener
masking or duct tape
acrylic paints
newspaper
sponge cut into small pieces
container of water
heavy string or wire
hanger, tree branch, or dowel

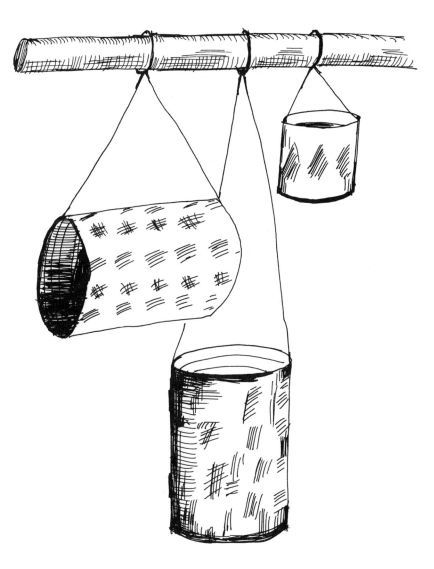

## PROCESS:
1. Peel off labels from tin cans and remove both ends with a can opener. Wash and dry. Tape over sharp edges with masking tape or duct tape.
2. Squeeze out acrylic paint onto newspaper.
3. Moisten sponge pieces in water and dip into acrylic paints. Dab color onto tin cans.
4. Let dry.
5. Run heavy string or wire through each can and fasten to hanger, tree branch, or dowel.

## VARIATIONS:
1. Hang decorated cans from heavy string or cording as a ceiling decoration.
2. Cover cans with recycled gift wrap or fabric instead of sponge printing.
3. Add dry flowers or paper flowers to cans as decoration.

# TOOTHPICK SCULPTURE

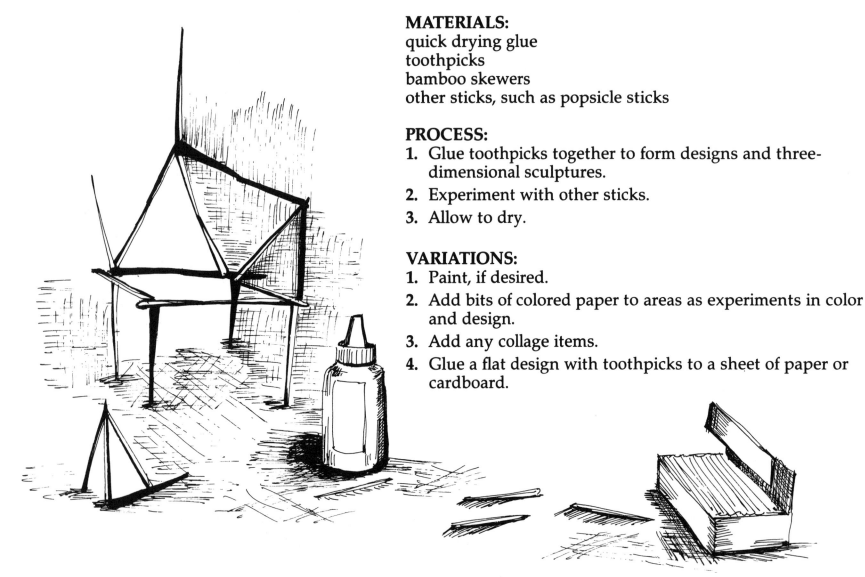

**MATERIALS:**
quick drying glue
toothpicks
bamboo skewers
other sticks, such as popsicle sticks

**PROCESS:**
1. Glue toothpicks together to form designs and three-dimensional sculptures.
2. Experiment with other sticks.
3. Allow to dry.

**VARIATIONS:**
1. Paint, if desired.
2. Add bits of colored paper to areas as experiments in color and design.
3. Add any collage items.
4. Glue a flat design with toothpicks to a sheet of paper or cardboard.

# FRAME SCULPTURE

## MATERIALS:
picture frame scraps
carpenter's glue
tempera paints (optional)
container of water
rags
brushes

## PROCESS:
1. Arrange picture frame scraps in an interesting way, and glue pieces together with carpenter's glue.
2. Let dry.
3. Paint, if desired.

## VARIATIONS:
1. Try making an animal or person from wood scraps.
2. Try making a city.
3. Have an adult supervise use of glue gun for rapid, strong sculpting.
4. Combine cardboard tubes and spools with framing scraps.
5. Use any wood scraps.

## MATERIALS:
1 cup of cinnamon
¼ cup of white glue
¼ to ½ cup of water
rolling pin
cookie cutters
straw or pencil
ornament hooks
ribbon
oven, preheated to 200°

## PROCESS:
1. Mix together all ingredients.
2. Roll out mixture onto a flat surface and cut with cookie cutters to make ornaments.
3. Poke a hole through each ornament with a straw or pencil for the ribbon.
4. **(CAUTION)** Place cinnamon ornaments in a warm oven.
5. Turn ornaments every 5 to 10 minutes until firm.
6. Place a ribbon through the cooled ornaments and tie the ribbon into a bow or knot.
7. Attach finished ornament on an ornament hook and hang on a tree branch or plant.

## VARIATIONS:
1. Add pinches of nutmeg and cloves to cinnamon.
2. Try modeling the mixture into coils or shapes by hand.

# THEME TREE

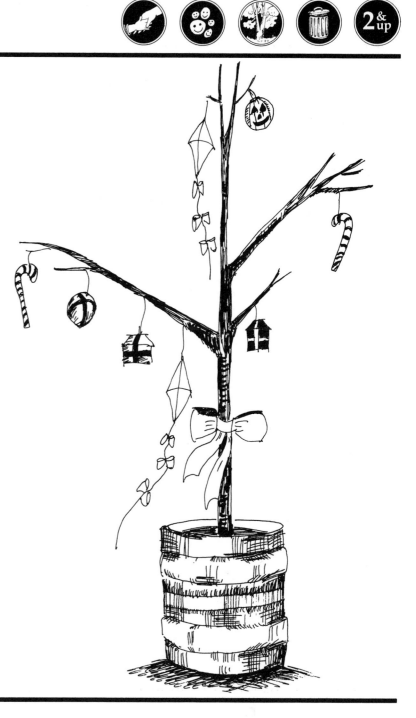

**MATERIALS:**
small branch
coffee can filled with sand
thread, string or yarn
items to hang on branch

**PROCESS:**
1. Fill a coffee can with sand for stability.
2. Stick a branch without leaves in the sand.
3. Decide how to decorate the branch. The decorations can be changed whenever you wish for the holidays, for special times, or whenever you have something pretty you've made to hang on the branches.

**VARIATIONS:**
1. Collect items from nature and hang from string.
2. Make paper decorations for a holiday theme.
3. Hang magazine pictures glued to heavy paper for a theme of happiness, fun times, protecting animals, favorite colors, or other themes you choose.
4. Save bits of machine parts or hardware items to hang.
5. What else? Did someone say "candy"?

# MODELING BEESWAX

**MATERIALS:**
modeling beeswax (available from craft stores)

**PROCESS:**
1. Soften beeswax (about ¼ stick) by holding in hands until it is warm and pliable.
2. Begin to shape the wax. Pull, roll, or flatten. Use imagination.
3. When wax cools, it hardens and keeps its shape.
4. To reuse wax, soften again and create something new.

**VARIATIONS:**
1. Pull thin wax petals to make delicate, translucent flowers.
2. Pull legs, neck, head, tail and ears from ball to make an animal.
3. Knead different colors of wax together for marbled effect.
4. Cover a cardboard cottage after kneading wax thin.
5. Make scenes such as an exotic flower garden, characters from a favorite story, or a fantasy land.

**NOTE:**
Modeling beeswax is wonderful because it is a natural gift of the earth and entirely unique from any commercial modeling compound. Available through: Hearth Song, P.O. Box B, Sebastopol, CA 95473, 1-800-325-2502, or ask your local orthodontist for a handful of dental wax.

*PS: Wax will melt. Do not leave beeswax in direct sunlight, in the car, or near a heat source.*

# BURDOCK FIGURES

**MATERIALS:**
burdocks (burrs) or cockleburrs

**PROCESS:**
1. Walk through an overgrown field.
2. Collect burdocks from your clothes or from the plants.
3. Stick burdocks to each other to make figures such as people, animals, shapes, or sculptures.
4. Burdocks will stick to each other with their little barbed stickers. (Burdocks inspired the invention of Velcro.)

**VARIATIONS:**
1. Add burdock figures to other nature sculptures or flower arrangements.
2. Glue on eyes, scraps of fabric, or other decorative items. Try adding other items from nature, too, with glue.

# SANDY BAKERY

**MATERIALS:**
sand
water
cookie cutters and cake pan
cupcake or muffin tins
cookie sheet or pizza pan
seeds, berries, grasses, twigs, small stones (optional)

**PROCESS:**
1. Moisten sand with water so that it can be molded by hand and holds its shape.
2. Pack sand into cake pan for sandy cookies or cupcake tins for sandy cupcakes.
3. Turn cupcake tin upside down on cookie sheet for sandy cupcakes. Use cookie cutters to cut out shapes from cake pan and turn sandy shape onto cookie sheet or pizza pan.
4. Leave plain or decorate with berries, grasses, twigs, dry sand, small stones or other natural objects.

**VARIATIONS:**
1. Build an imaginary cake sculpture with cans, buckets, containers.
2. Try using one of the cake pans formed as characters, animals, or whimsical shapes.
3. Form cookies, cakes, and treats by hand.

# SNOWY BAKERY

**MATERIALS:**
snow
cookie cutters and cake pan
cupcake or muffin tins
cookie sheet or pizza pan
food coloring or colored sugar (optional)

**PROCESS:**
1. Pack snow into cake pan for snowy cookies or cupcake tins for snowy cupcakes. (Use clean, untouched snow.)
2. Turn cupcake tin upside down on cookie sheet for snowy cupcakes. Use cookie cutters to cut out shapes from cake pan and turn snowy shapes onto cookie sheet or pizza pan.
3. Leave plain or decorate with food coloring or colored sugar.

**VARIATIONS:**
1. Spray snowy baked goods with food coloring and water mixture in clean spray bottle.
2. Make wedding cake outside with variety of pans and containers. Pack firmly.
3. Form cookies, cakes, and treats by hand.

# PINE CONE SCULPTURES

**MATERIALS:**
pine cones
white glue
crayons or markers
pencils
string or thread

**PROCESS:**
1. Pine cone should be dry and free of dirt.
2. Cut out odd shapes and designs from your paper.
3. Add decorations to shapes with pencils, markers, and crayons.
4. Attach shapes to pine cone with white glue.
5. Let dry.
6. Hang up pine cone sculpture with string or thread.

**VARIATIONS:**
1. Make a pine cone critter.
2. Make a pine cone person.
3. Make a pine cone mobile by hanging several pine cones from a stick.
4. Display sculptures, critters, or people on a stick of driftwood, discarded brick, or 2x4 wood scrap.

# SEASHELL DISPLAYS

**MATERIALS:**
seashells in assorted shapes, sizes and colors
paper scraps
scissors
white glue
pencils, crayons, or markers

**PROCESS:**
1. Make sure that the seashells are clean, dry and free of dirt and sand.
2. Use scissors and paper scraps to create shapes and designs.
3. Color paper pieces and glue to shells.
4. The unique shell and paper structure is your Seashell Display.

**VARIATIONS:**
1. Try making sea people, mermaids, fish, reptiles, or creatures from shells.
2. Try adding broken jewelry, beads, buttons, or other items for decoration.

# ON-SITE BEACH ART

**MATERIALS:**
natural items collected at the beach such as —

| | |
|---|---|
| glass | dry grasses and reeds |
| shells | seaweed |
| pods | driftwood |
| sand | |

**PROCESS:**
1. Pick up interesting items and bring to a spot on the beach where you will work.
2. Lay out the items and begin to create a design, a face, a picture, or a collage on the sand.
3. Move parts around as you go.
4. Go back and look for more items to add to your work.
5. Leave on the beach as is, or glue to a piece of cardboard to take home.

**VARIATIONS:**
1. Make a trash collection picture. Leave visible for others to see, and then clean-up and recycle appropriately when you go home.
2. Build a beach sculpture that stands up, using logs, wood, and other larger beach items.
3. Try this same project at the park, the school playground, the mountains, the pond, or in your own backyard.
4. Glue smaller items to a piece of driftwood or shell.
5. Make on-site desert art, forest art, playground art, or backyard art. Any environment can be on-site art.

# NATURE BOX

**MATERIALS:**
half of gift box
paper
scissors
glue, stapler, or tape
strips of heavy paper
nature collectables such as:

    beach glass      coral
    pebbles         nuts and seeds
    shells          etc.
    bits of driftwood

**PROCESS:**
1. Place strips of paper in gift box in such a way as to make little compartments or sections. Staple, glue, or tape. (Hint: It helps to fold back the ends of the strips to attach to the walls of the box.)
2. Glue treasured collections into the small sections.

**VARIATIONS:**
1. Make a beach collection.
2. Make a forest collection.
3. Take a walk and collect things just for the display box.
4. Paint background of box before making walls.
5. Glue pretty paper to box before making walls.
6. Use an egg carton instead of making a box.
7. Use a large sectioned cardboard box suitable for a larger collection of rocks and chunks of driftwood.

**MATERIALS:**
piece of a log, wood, or driftwood
white glue
small objects gathered from nature such as:
   pine cones    bracket fungi
   leaves       small branches
paper
scissors
markers or crayons
paints and brush

**PROCESS:**
1. Glue natural objects such as pine cones and leaves or small branches and twigs on a piece of wood.
2. Use paints or markers to add design.
3. Cut out paper and glue onto the art design, if desired.

**VARIATIONS:**
**Try making a nature scene on a piece of wood —**
1. Use branches, twigs, and pine cones to represent grass and trees.
2. Use paints to create rivers or lakes.
3. Add cut-out animals, people, or buildings.

# DRIFTWOOD SCULPTURE

**MATERIALS:**
assorted seashells, coral and small pieces of driftwood
larger piece of driftwood
white glue

**PROCESS:**
1. Spread white glue over seashells, coral, and bits of wood.
2. Stick on large piece of driftwood.
3. Cover the driftwood with a seashell arrangement.
4. Let dry.

Suggestion: Only collect shells and coral which are empty or dead. Never take live animals from the beach.

**VARIATIONS:**
1. Cover a cigar box or jewelry gift box with shells.
2. Add other items such as beach glass, pebbles, sand, and dry seeds or grasses from the beach to the sculpture.
3. Use a large clam shell as a base and glue on smaller shells and beach items.

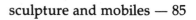

# NEST CONSTRUCTION

**MATERIALS:**
dried grasses, twigs
scraps of paper
bits of trash
yard or string
cotton fluff or cattail fluff
feathers or down
mud

**PROCESS:**
1. Build a nest much like the birds do.
2. Form a nest shape using mud to bind, weaving your materials together.
3. Line nest with fluff or feathers, just like the birds.
4. Allow nest to dry.
5. Enjoy your construction just like a decoration.

**VARIATIONS:**
1. Make eggs and add to nest.
2. Make a bird and add to nest.
3. Dye real eggs and add to nest.

# NATURE MOBILE

## MATERIALS:
branch or stick
natural collected objects such as:

| | | | |
|---|---|---|---|
| pebbles | leaves | twigs | apples |
| pine cones | wildflowers | nuts | mushrooms |

string, twine, or thread

## PROCESS:
1. Tie collected nature objects to branch or stick with twine, string, or thread.
2. Tie twine or string onto branch to hang.
   (Hint: You may need more than one piece for balance.)

## VARIATIONS:
**Try a theme mobile:**
1. feather mobile
2. wildflower mobile
3. pine cone mobile
4. seaside mobile
5. woods mobile
6. autumn mobile
7. "My Nature Walk" mobile

# ELDERBERRY WIND CHIMES

**MATERIALS:**
elderberry wood (or other hollow wood, like sumac)
wire coat hanger
saw
yarn or string

**PROCESS:**
CAUTION
1. Find elderberry or other hollow wood. Cut into pieces 1″ -6″.
2. Push the pith out with a straightened wire coat hanger.
3. String these pieces and hang from a larger branch.
4. Allow chimes to blow in the wind.

**VARIATIONS:**
**Wind chimes can be made from a variety of materials, combined or used alone. Some suggestions are:**
1. metal chimes from washers or nails
2. shell chimes, especially jingle shells
3. cans, pieces of wood, or metal pipes

# SEASHELL CHIMES

## MATERIALS:
shells        electric drill        driftwood or branch
strong colored yarn    scissors

## PROCESS:
1. Drill hole in one end of each shell. (Adult must do this step for younger child and assist older child.)
2. Cut yarn to lengths for hanging from branch.
3. Hang branch between two chairs.
4. Tie yarn to branch in different spots, keeping yarn strands close enough together to touch when the wind blows.
5. Thread shells to the yarn.
6. Add more than one shell to each piece of yarn, leaving spaces between.
   (Note: Knot between shells to prevent slipping.)
7. Thread and knot shells onto other pieces of yarn.
   (Hint: Be sure to space the weight of the shells evenly so branch will balance.)
8. Check to be sure shells will bump each other when the wind blows.

## VARIATIONS:
1. Make a chime from chunks of scrap wood. (Ask a shop teacher to save the funny little pieces from the jig saw.)
2. Ask a frame shop owner to save pieces of framing for you to use for chimes.
3. Tie nuts, bolts, and nails to yarn for a wind chime.

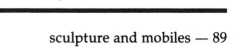

# PEBBLE TOWERS

**MATERIALS:**
smooth pebbles
white glue
pie tin (saved from frozen pot-pie)

**PROCESS:**
1. After turning pie tin upside down, press a dent in the tin and fill with glue.
2. Place largest pebbles into dent.
3. Dry completely.
4. Put a drop of glue on each pebble and dry a few minutes.
5. Add a layer of smaller pebbles to the tacky glue.
6. Dry completely.
7. Continue adding drops of glue, drying, and adding layers of smaller pebbles, and drying completely between layers.

**VARIATIONS:**
1. Paint sculptures with white glue for a glossy finish.
2. Make many sculptures and place together for a scene of towers from a rock fantasy land, outer space, or under the sea.
3. Several children can combine towers to make one large sculpture.

# TOTEM POLE

**MATERIALS:**
log
tempera paints or latex paints
paintbrushes
rags
container filled with water

**PROCESS:**
1. Make sure log is dry and free of dirt and insects.
2. Paint log in sections.
3. Use a different face or design in each section from the top to the bottom.
4. Let dry.
5. Display totem pole in a standing position.

**VARIATIONS:**
1. Paint a log in any design. Try designs of all circles and squares, or all birds for a theme idea.
2. Carve log first, then paint.
3. Make totem pole by stacking cardboard boxes or ice cream containers instead of a log.
4. Make a log totem pole without paint, using items from nature to decorate faces.

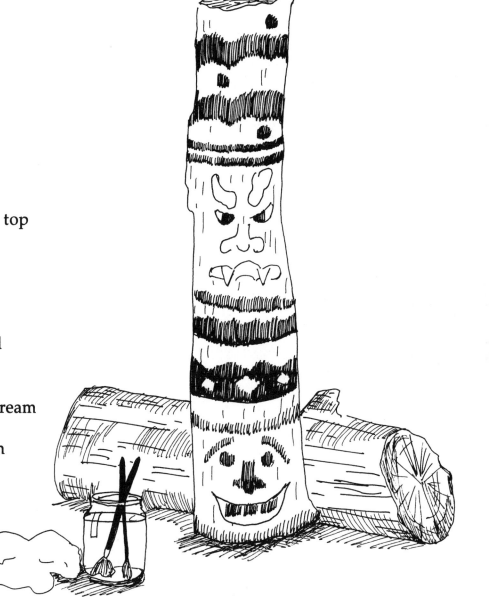

# CHEESE CARVING

**MATERIALS:**
block of hard cheese such as cheddar
wire cheese cutter
potato peeler
butter knife
toothpick
fork

### RECIPE 1: Relief
**PROCESS:**
1. Use the toothpick to draw a picture or a design into the cheese.
2. Use the wire cheese cutter, potato peeler, butter knife and fork to dig out the background of your picture or design and create interesting textures in the cheese.

### RECIPE 2: Intaglio
**PROCESS:**
1. Lightly draw a design or picture onto the cheese with a toothpick or potato peeler.
2. Use the potato peeler, butter knife, wire cheese cutter, and fork to dig out your design or picture from the background, and create interesting textures in the cheese.

**NOTE:**
Please eat food sculptures soon after creating.
Save the pared-away cheese scraps for salad, pets, or snacks.

# SCULPTURE SALAD

**MATERIALS:**
leaf of lettuce, washed and dried
choices of food:
   peach or pear
   banana
   celery stick
   carrot stick or circles
   hard-cooked egg
   raisins
   grapes

**PROCESS:**
1. Wash hands.
2. Lay leaf on plate.
3. Assemble fruits and veggies into a design, figure, or animal.
4. Decorate until it's ready.
5. Eat and enjoy, or serve to someone special.

**VARIATIONS:**
**Design a sculpture salad for a special occasion, such as:**
1. a pretty sunshine from a peach for the first day of summer
2. cottage cheese with dots of cherries or strawberries, molded in a heart shape for Valentine's Day
3. a candle made from a banana with a cherry flame for a winter holiday
4. cheese circles cut with faces for Halloween

# GARDEN CRITTERS

**MATERIALS:**

one or more of the following fruits or vegetables: apple, potato, pear, cucumber, peach, nectarine, plum, sweet potato

small knife · paintbrush
white glue · container of water
scissors · rags
tempera paint · newspaper
collected optional natural objects such as:

| small twigs | seeds | pinecones | bark |
| pebbles | nuts | feathers | |

**PROCESS:**

1. Make sure your natural collected objects are dry and free of dirt and insects.

2. Spread newapaper over a flat surface and place your fruit or vegetable on the newspaper.

3. Use small twigs to create arms and legs by pushing them into the fruit or vegetable.

4. Use other natural objects to create heads, clothes, and other details.
   (Hint: Do this by gluing them on with white glue or carving out a tiny hole and pushing seeds and pebbles into the hole.)

5. Use scissors to trim twigs or feathers as needed. Let dry.

6. Use paintbrush and tempera paint to add a face and other details to your vegetable or fruit critter.

**VARIATION:**

Assemble your critter with only edible decorations. Use as a snack or salad.

# COLLAGE AND PRINTING

chapter 3

# CARDBOARD COLLAGE

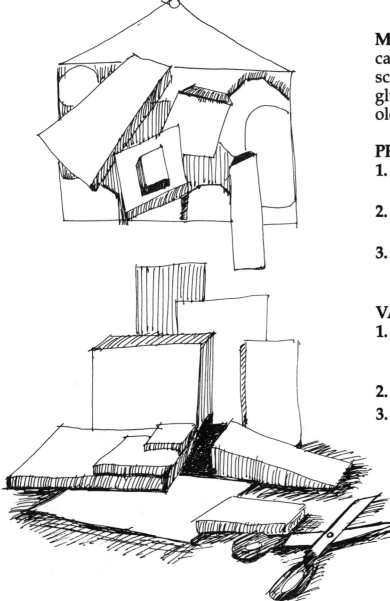

**MATERIALS:**
cardboard, 1 large piece and other scraps
scissors
glue
old magazines and interesting scraps, optional

**PROCESS:**
1. Cut and glue scraps of cardboard to larger cardboard background.
2. Build up several layers for interesting three-dimensional effect, some high, some low.
3. Add magazine pictures or other interesting bits of paper to highlight areas of color and design in the collage.

**VARIATIONS:**
1. Cover entire design with aluminum foil, pressing and rubbing to show shapes and designs of cardboard underneath.
2. Paint each piece of cardboard for a quilted effect.
3. Try this same project using scraps of wood on a larger wooden or cardboard background.

# STRING COLLAGE

**MATERIALS:**
save scraps of string, yarn, cord
liquid starch
cardboard
tray or bowl
scissors

**PROCESS:**
1. Cut yarn or string into 1 ft. lengths.
2. Soak in tray filled with liquid starch.
3. Pull one starch-filled string out of tray and arrange on cardboard in a design.
4. Repeat with different colored strings and yarns.
5. Allow to dry overnight.

**VARIATIONS:**
1. String collage can be made on wallpaper, paper plates, old posters or wrapping paper.
2. Make on glass or foil, and peel off when dry. May be hung in window.
3. Add other items to string collage such as beads and buttons.

# PIZZA PUZZLES

**MATERIALS:**

| | |
|---|---|
| pizza box | glue stick |
| pizza circle | white glue |
| magazine pictures | scissors |

**PROCESS:**
1. Cut magazine pictures of food, and glue to pizza circle to resemble a real or imaginary pizza.
2. Coat with a layer of white glue.
3. Dry overnight until clear and hard.
4. Cut pizza circle into puzzle pieces of about 6-8 pieces. (It's fun to cut wedges which fit back together like real pizza.)
5. Put pizza puzzle back together in pizza box and keep in box for storage.

**VARIATIONS:**
1. Make any kind of puzzle on any shape of cardboard and cut into pieces.
2. Glue a solid magazine picture to a piece of cardboard, and then cut into wiggly strips instead of pieces.
3. Cut puzzle pieces from other items such as cereal boxes, cookie boxes, photographs, posters, or coloring books.
4. Cover any puzzle with clear contact before cutting into pieces for a longer lasting puzzle.
5. Store puzzles in old file folders stapled or taped up the sides, in envelopes, or in small boxes saved from gifts.

# MATCH BOX PUZZLE

**MATERIALS:**
sheet of paper
empty match boxes
felt tipped pens
scissors
white glue
ruler
drawing

**PROCESS:**
1. Select a drawing.
2. Using a ruler, mark off the match box size on back of drawing. An 8"x10" drawing will take about 12 match boxes to fill the drawing.
3. Following the lines, cut out the match box shapes of the drawing, and glue one to each match box.
4. Arrange the boxes to make a puzzle of the original drawing.

**VARIATIONS:**
1. Make box puzzles from:
      recycled wrapping
      favorite photographs
      old posters
      magazine pictures
2. First cover match boxes with plain paper, and then draw on each one.

# MECHANICAL CONTRAPTION

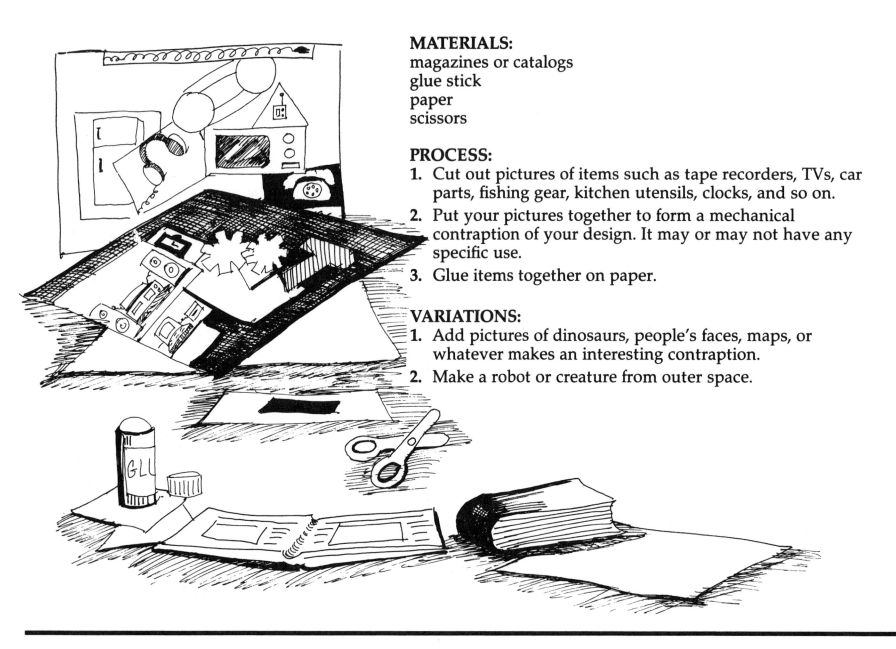

**MATERIALS:**
magazines or catalogs
glue stick
paper
scissors

**PROCESS:**
1. Cut out pictures of items such as tape recorders, TVs, car parts, fishing gear, kitchen utensils, clocks, and so on.
2. Put your pictures together to form a mechanical contraption of your design. It may or may not have any specific use.
3. Glue items together on paper.

**VARIATIONS:**
1. Add pictures of dinosaurs, people's faces, maps, or whatever makes an interesting contraption.
2. Make a robot or creature from outer space.

# EASY DÉCOUPAGE

**MATERIALS:**
white glue
magazine pictures
heavy paper, paper plate, or gift box
paint brush

**PROCESS:**
**Découpage is a way of coating objects with a hard, glossy finish to make decorations.**
1. Coat heavy paper with white glue.
2. Stick selected magazine pictures into glue.
3. Cover with another layer of white glue.
4. Dry.
5. Coat with another layer of white glue.
6. Dry completely. (The white glue will dry clear and hard.)

**VARIATIONS:**
1. Découpage flowers, ferns, or other dried items from nature.
2. Découpage photographs.
3. Découpage wrapping paper, greeting cards, or any paper cut into designs.

# SEED WIGGLES

**MATERIALS:**
white glue
wax paper
seeds
spoon
bag
string

**PROCESS:**
1. Squeeze a line of white glue on a sheet of wax paper. Make the line nice and wide and even, not lumpy.
2. Sprinkle seeds over the glue with a spoon, covering all the glue.
3. Dry overnight.
4. Shake off loose seeds into bag to use for other projects.
5. Gently peel the seed wiggle from the paper.
   (Adult may need to help with this step.)
6. Tie string to the seed wiggle to hang in window or from ceiling.

**VARIATIONS:**
1. Make the alphabet in glue and seeds.
2. Make planned shapes and designs instead of wiggles.
3. Hang several wiggles from a stick or hanger for a mobile.

# WOOD SHAVINGS COLLAGE

**MATERIALS:**
wood shavings from all types of wood
   (ask a shop teacher, a lumber yard, or a construction site)
white glue
cardboard
paint and paintbrush, optional

**PROCESS:**
1. Glue a variety of wood shavings to cardboard.
2. When collage is dry, wood shavings can be painted.

**VARIATIONS:**
1. Before gluing shavings, cut cardboard into any shapes you
   like, such as:
       animals
       buildings
       wreaths
       pretty shapes, and so on
2. Add other items to collage such as:
       buttons
       seeds
       nuts or
       paper cut-outs

# PUT-TOGETHERS

**MATERIALS:**
cardboard, tag, or poster board
white glue
scissors
collected items such as:

| | | |
|---|---|---|
| grass | popsicle sticks | bark |
| wildflowers | seeds | pine needles |
| twigs | buttons | string |
| matchsticks | pebbles | pop bottle caps |

pencils, markers or crayons

**PROCESS:**
1. Cut out a shape from the piece of cardboard or poster board.
2. Glue collected items to the cardboard to create designs and patterns.
3. Let dry.
4. Use markers, pencils or crayons to add details.

**VARIATIONS:**
1. Create a put-together creature or animal.
2. Create a put-together person. Create a suite and tie, bathing suit, football uniform or costume. Include shoes, jewelry, and other ideas.

# DRIED BEAN PICTURES

**MATERIALS:**
dried beans such as:
   dry kidney beans
   white beans
   navy beans
   split peas or
   corn
cardboard square
white glue
crayons
pencil

**PROCESS:**
1. Draw a picture or design on the paper lightly in pencil.
2. Apply glue on the pencil lines.
3. Arrange beans on wet glue.
4. Let dry.
5. Use crayons to add detail or more color to the creations.

**VARIATIONS:**
1. Use small pebbles, macaroni, or colored sand instead of beans.
2. Glue beans on a scrap of wood instead of cardboard.

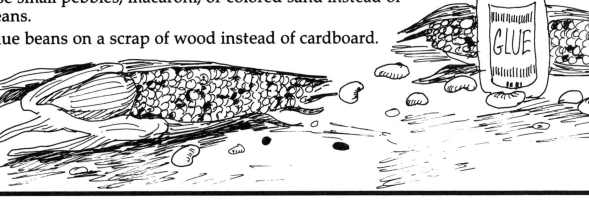

**MATERIALS:**
waxed paper
leaves (either fresh or dry)
iron
newspaper
scissors

**PROCESS:**
1. Spread newspaper over a flat surface.
2. Place a square piece of waxed paper on the newspaper.
3. Arrange leaves on the waxed paper. (Make sure that none of the leaves touch the edge of the waxed paper.)
4. Place another piece of waxed paper on top of the leaves.
5. Cover this with another layer of newspaper.
6. Press waxed paper leaf collage with a warm iron. 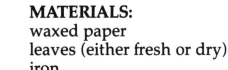 (CAUTION)
7. Remove newspaper.
8. Trim off the rough edges of waxed paper with scissors.
9. Place collage in a window and watch the light shine through the beautiful leaves.

**VARIATIONS:**
1. Add confetti, lace, glitter, ribbon, or bits of colored paper.
2. Make a leaf banner with 2 very long pieces of waxed paper.

# SANDWICH BAG DESIGNS

**MATERIALS:**
plastic sandwich bags
items to put inside:
    glitter
    stars
    confetti
    fabric shapes
    lace
    ribbon
aluminum foil
iron
scissors

**PROCESS:**
1. Put items for your design inside bag.
   (Hint: leave some areas open so plastic will stick together.)
2. Put design bag between two sheets of aluminum foil.
3. Press foil with warm iron. **CAUTION**
4. Peel away foil.
5. Trim plastic to a shape if you like.

**VARIATIONS:**
1. Do this same project with waxed paper sandwich bags, and press between newsprint instead of foil.
2. Try adding grated crayons or powdered chalk.
3. Try adding little bits of cut up greeting cards or wrapping paper.
4. Try using leaves or pressed flowers instead of scrap items.

# FOIL ART

## MATERIALS:

light weight cardboard
white glue
string or yarn
heavy duty foil
black tempera (mixed with liquid detergent)

pin backs, optional
scissors
paint brush
steel wool
paper clip, optional

## PROCESS:

1. Cut a cardboard shape such as an oval, circle, square, or triangle. Smooth edges work best.
2. Coat one side of the cardboard with glue.
3. Place string or yarn on glue in a design.
4. Cut a piece of foil large enough to cover the string design and over edges to back of cardboard. (No cardboard should show on back.)
5. Coat dull side of foil with glue.
6. Stick glue side to string and cardboard.
7. Wrap excess foil around to cover the back of the design.
8. Rub the design side to bring up the design. (Use fingers or try using an eraser of a pencil.)
9. Paint the front with black paint mixed with liquid detergent. (Detergent helps paint stick to foil.) Dry.
10. Rub the design with steel wool to shine the string bumps.
11. Coat the front and back with a layer of white glue and allow to dry overnight. Add a paper clip for hanging or a hobby pin to the back for wearing.

## VARIATION:

Cover an entire box with glue, designs, and foil to make a gift box.

# FUNNY-PAPER ART

**MATERIALS:**
comic books, Sunday paper comics, or magazines
thin cardboard
white glue
scissors
paintbrush

**PROCESS:**
1. Cut out a small picture.
2. Cut the cardboard to the size and shape of the picture.
3. Paint the back of the picture with glue.
4. Stick picture to cardboard, pressing out wrinkles a bit.
5. Paint a layer of glue over entire picture.
6. When dry, give picture another coat of glue.
   (Note: Glue acts as a glossy, clear, hard finish.)

**VARIATIONS:**
1. Cut a picture small enough to work as a pin. Glue a pin
   back to the back of the picture. Wear.
2. Glue picture to a cardboard box as decoration. Coat box
   with glue, too.
3. Glue picture or a series of pictures to a scrap of wood in a
   stand-up position.

# BEAN JAR

**MATERIALS:**
large jar with lid, washed and dried
spoon
assortment of dried beans:
    lentils
    kidney beans
    peas or
    other died beans

**PROCESS:**
1. Spoon in the first layer of one kind of beans. Make it as deep as you like.
2. Spoon in the second layer of a different kind of beans on top of the first layer.
3. Keep spooning layers until the jar is full.
4. Put on lid.
5. Set in window or on shelf to enjoy.

**VARIATIONS:**
1. Use macaroni and pretty pastas as some of the layers.
2. Make a layered jar with different colors of sand.
3. Mix uncooked rice with food coloring. Make several colors. Dry. Use for colored layers in a jar.
4. Add decoration to the jar, if you like.

# SANDS OF MANY COLORS

**MATERIALS:**
sand
food coloring or tempera paints
glass jar with a lid
several cups or containers
fork
butter knife

**PROCESS:**
1. Place sand in cups and add a few drops of food coloring or a few drops of tempera paint.
2. Stir with fork. Each cup will be a different color.
3. Dry briefly.
4. Pour colored sand into glass jar in layers of different colors. Use a butter knife to create mounds and valleys along the sides of the glass.
5. Place lid on top of your sands of many colors.

**VARIATIONS:**
1. Try using different shapes and sizes of jars.
2. Try layering sand with small shells or smooth pebbles pushed against the glass.
3. Add dry Jell-o, Kool-Aid, or powdered drink mixes for a variety of colored layers.
4. Use sand like glitter on paintings, on glue designs, or sprinkle on paper for temporary drawings.

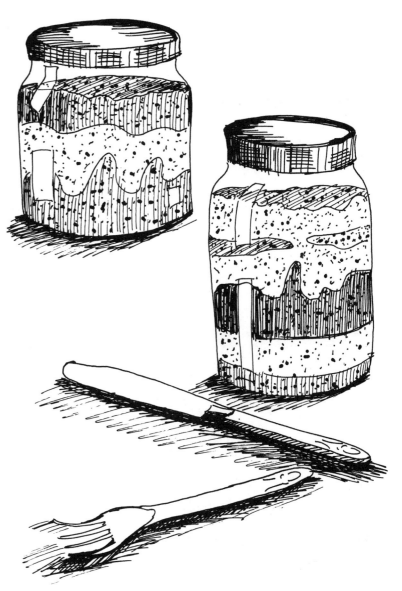

# YARN PRINTS

**MATERIALS:**

colorful yarn scraps                         scissors
glue                                         paint
cardboard or mat board (from frame shop)     paper for printing

**PROCESS:**

1. Measure and fold cardboard into thirds.
2. Tape open side of cardboard, forming a triangle or tent shape.
3. Glue yarn shapes to two of three sides and dry.
4. When dry, glue yarn to third side and dry.
5. Press yarn design into paint on a plate or in meat tray.
6. Press painted design onto paper for a print of the design.
7. Continue printing until satisfied with design.

**VARIATIONS:**

1. Paint yarn design with brush filled with paint instead of dipping design in paint.
2. "Roll" tent-shaped printer so that all three sides print in succession.
3. Make wrapping paper.
4. Use printer's ink instead of paint.
5. Make a small version of the tent, and use to decorate note cards or stationery.
6. Use a cardboard tube instead of the triangle.
7. Use a block of wood instead of the tube or triangle.

# JUNK PRINTING

**MATERIALS:**
collect any or all of the following:
- nuts
- bolts
- toys
- corks
- kitchen utensils
- car parts
- tools
- rubber stamps
- paper clips
- coins
- jar lids
- film containers

ink pads
paper

**PROCESS:**
1. Press junk item into ink pad.
2. Press inked junk onto paper.
3. Repeat or change junk item.
4. Continue printing.
5. Try for a pattern or enjoy random design shapes.

**VARIATIONS:**
1. Print with paint instead of ink.
2. Try using food coloring on a paper towel for a pad.
3. Make wrapping paper or decorate stationery.
4. Scour construction sites, garage sales, or thrift shops for unusual junk items.

# EASY SUN PRINT

**MATERIALS:**
leaf
colored construction paper (or other soft colored paper)
bright sunshine
sewing pins or rocks

**PROCESS:**
1. Pin leaves to colored paper, or weight with rocks.
   (Note: For best leaf prints, rocks should not extend over edges of leaves.)
2. Place in sunshine for about 1 hour.
3. Remove from sunshine and remove leaves.
4. The silhouette will be left.

**VARIATIONS:**
1. Make sun prints of toys, tools, utensils.
2. Try for a planned design made from cutting cardboard or paper shapes.
3. Try making "name sun prints" from the letters of the alphabet pre-cut and arranged on the colored paper.

# SOLAR PRINTS

**MATERIALS:**
sun-printing paper, from hobby shops and museum shops
leaves, flowers, or any items you choose
sunlight
water in flat pan

**PROCESS:**
1. Arrange your items on sun-printing paper. Be careful not to move things once they are on the paper.
2. Expose the paper to sunlight for about five minutes.
3. Remove objects.
4. Immediately put paper in water to "fix" the image so it will be permanent.

**VARIATIONS:**
1. Cut designs out and glue to folded note card paper.
2. Frame your prints or hang them.
3. Trace around outlines and color the images.
4. Make a collage of solar prints.
5. Try using toys, tools, nuts and bolts, cut cardboard shapes (letters, too?), and other imaginative shapes to make solar prints.
6. Experiment with colored construction paper, but no need to dip in water. Simply remove from sunlight.

# INNERTUBE PRINTS

**MATERIALS:**
scraps of wood (blocks work well)
piece of rubber from innertube
tacky glue
scissors
ink pad

**PROCESS:**

1. Cut innertube rubber into desired shapes and designs.
2. Glue one shape on each block of wood. Dry overnight.
3. Press stamp on ink pad and make design on paper.

**VARIATIONS:**
1. If ink pad is dry or old, re-ink with food coloring mixed with a little water.
2. No ink pad? Use food coloring on paper towels.
3. Paint shape with paint-filled brush — then stamp on paper.
4. Is a wall design a possiblity? Experiment on a closet wall before starting on noticeable area.

# ROLLER PRINTING CANS

## MATERIALS:
large juice can, oatmeal box, or grits box
heavy dowel
felt weather stripping scraps (or cardboard, or styrofoam)
rubber cement
paper
tempera paint
shallow pan

## PROCESS:
1. Punch a hole in each end of the can or box, next pushing dowel through.
2. Cut out shapes from felt, foam, or cardboard.
3. Cover the entire sides of can or box with rubber cement and let dry.
4. Glue shapes to sides of can or box.
5. Pour paint in pan.
6. Roll can through paint.
7. Roll can over paper.

## VARIATIONS:
1. Heavy cardboard tube can be used instead of can or box.
2. Experiment with designs that go all the way around the cylinder.
3. Try gluing yarn or heavy cord in fun designs to cylinder.

# STENCIL PRINTS

## MATERIALS:
old file folders          ink pads
scissors or X-acto knife          fingers

## PROCESS:
1. Cut stencils from old file folders with scissors.
   Note: Only older children should use an X-acto knife.  (CAUTION)
2. Place stencil over paper to be decorated or printed.
3. Hold firmly.
4. Press finger tips onto brightly colored ink pads or color finger tips with felt pens.
5. Press colored finger tips over stencil. Use several colors, one on top of another, if desired.
6. Remove stencil and move to another area of paper.
7. Repeat.

## VARIATIONS:
1. From a printer or graphic artist, ask for backing from Rubylith. Cut a stencil from the backing with an X-acto knife, bend, and pop out. Repeat above printing process.
2. Try using the pieces of stencil that were removed, and repeat the printing process with an opposite effect.
3. Make note cards, wrapping paper, or pretty designs just to enjoy.

## NOTE:
With very young children, adult cuts the stencil and child does the rest.

# SCREEN PRINT

**MATERIALS:**

embroidery hoop

piece of cheese cloth large enough to cover hoop

stapler

heavy paper, such as tag board

tongue depressor

paper

scissors

finger paint

**PROCESS:**

1. To make the "screen", stretch 2 or 3 layers of cheese cloth between hoops.
2. Cut any design from tag board with scissors, watching that design fits within the size of the hoop.
3. Lay a piece of paper on the table.
4. Place stencil on paper.
5. Place screen on top of stencil.
6. Drop some finger paint (consistency of toothpaste) in hoop on screen.
7. Hold hoop with one hand, and scrape the paint across the stencil with a tongue depressor (short enough to fit inside hoop).
8. Gently lift the stencil and hoop, making sure the stencil remains adhered to the cheese cloth.
9. Repeat steps 3 through 8 for another print. Work rapidly so paint does not dry and clog cheese cloth.

**VARIATIONS:**

1. Try cutting a stencil, then coloring in the cut area with colored chalk. Brush chalk with tissue before removing stencil to smooth the image. Then remove stencil.
2. Cut a stencil, and press inked fingertips over stencil cuts to color those areas.

# CHALK FLOATS

**MATERIALS:**
paper or mat board
dish pan
water colored chalk
cheese grater

**PROCESS:**
1. Fill dish pan with water.
2. Grate or crush chalk sticks into powder. (Use old pieces that were on their way out, anyway.)
3. Sprinkle chalk on water in pan.
4. Lay paper or mat board on top of water to soak up chalk design.
5. Gently lift paper off water, and design will stick to paper.
6. Allow paper to dry.

**VARIATIONS:**
1. Instead of chalk, drop oil-based ink on top of water. Swirl. Lay paper on water, then peel off with design.
2. Spray or drip enamel paint on water in bucket or pan. Swirl with stick. Dip paper or old file folders into water and remove with marbled design transferred to paper.

# BUBBLE POP ART

**MATERIALS:**
liquid detergent (Dawn works well)
straws
cups
colored paper
crayons or colored pens

**PROCESS:**
1. Mix a little detergent and water in a cup.
2. Dip the end of a straw into the cup and blow bubbles. (Note: Do not breathe in, but if you do, don't worry about it. It just tastes terrible, but won't really hurt you.)
3. Catch the bubbles on the colored paper.
4. When the bubbles pop, a wet circle will be left on the paper.
5. Draw around the wet outline, and make designs with crayons or colored pens.

**VARIATIONS:**
1. Mix paint into bubble soap for a colorful print.
2. Set cup in center of white paper. Blow continuously and allow bubbles to billow over cup and onto paper for hundreds of bubble designs.

# CUP STAMPS

## MATERIALS:

styrofoam cup with lid (washed, dry)   paper
styrofoam meat trays (washed, dry)   pen
white glue   scissors
stamp pad

## PROCESS:

1. Collect a cup and lid from a fast food restaurant or espresso bar. Wash and dry.
2. Save styrofoam meat tray from store purchase.
3. Turn cup upside down on tray, tracing around the open end of the cup with a pen.
4. Cut out the circle.
5. Draw a design on the circle with a pen.
6. Glue the circle with the drawing onto the lid for the cup.
7. Dry.
8. Coat the circle design with ink from a stamp pad (or tempera paint).
9. Press the inked design onto paper.

## VARIATIONS:

1. Try cutting any fancy shape from the tray and gluing it to the cup lid.
2. Repeat this project by gluing shapes to the push-up stick of a frozen yogurt pop.
3. Remember that food coloring works in place of paint or ink.

# GARDEN PRINTS

**MATERIALS:**
choose one of the following:   apple,   potato,   cucumber,   pear
small knife, spoon or tool
   (young children use a nail, screwdriver, or any digging tool)
paper                  container of water
tempera paint         rags
paintbrush

**PROCESS:**
1.  Cut the fruit or vegetable in half.   (CAUTION)
    (Note: Adults help young children.)
2.  Cut a design or picture into the soft part of the fruit or
    vegetable.
    (Hint: Try carving the design or picture so that it stands
    out from the rest of the fruit or vegetable. To do this, carve
    away the background with a knife. Or dig out the
    background with a small spoon.)
3.  Brush paint on the cut design.
4.  Press the painted vegetable/fruit onto paper.
5.  Lift and repeat.

**VARIATIONS:**
1.  Create a vegetable/fruit print banner by cutting paper into
    a long rectangle and adding a stick, branch, or hanger to
    the top and bottom. (Loop the paper over and fasten with
    masking tape.)
2.  Make your own wrapping paper.
3.  Try celery heart, oranges, corn on the cob, cabbage, and
    eggplant. Enjoy the pattern without carving.

# LEAF PRINTS

**MATERIALS:**
fresh green leaves
tempera paints
paintbrush
paper
jar of water
rags
newspaper

**PROCESS:**
1. Spread newspaper on a flat surface.
2. Place fresh green leaves on newspaper.
3. Paint one side of the leaves with tempera paints.
4. Arrange leaves on paper with the paint side down on the paper.
5. Place another piece of newspaper on top of the painted leaves and rub over the leaves with your hands.
   (Hint: Feel the leaves with your fingers underneath the newspaper.)
6. Lift up the newspaper and painted leaves. An impression of the leaves is left on the paper.
7. Display leaf prints or give as gifts.

**VARIATIONS:**
1. Try making leaf print wrapping paper or a banner.
2. Try making greeting cards.

# IRONED LEAF DESIGNS

**MATERIALS:**
fresh leaves
crayons
fabric or paper, 2 pieces
iron

**PROCESS:**
1. Color the back of a fresh leaf with crayons.
   (Hint: Blending several colors has a pretty effect.)
2. Place colored side down on fabric or paper.
3. Cover with another piece of fabric or paper.
4. Iron with a warm iron, transferring the crayon to the paper or fabric.
5. Remove leaf.

**VARIATIONS:**
1. Stretch fabric leaf deign in an embroidery hoop to display.
2. Glue paper leaf designs to poster board or tape in a window.

# FOILED LEAF PRINTS

**MATERIALS:**
leaves
aluminum foil
cardboard, scissors (optional)

**PROCESS:**
1. Place a leaf on the table.
2. Cover leaf with heavy duty aluminum foil.
3. Press and rub the foil until the print of the leaf shows through.
4. Cut out leaf print and glue to cardboard, if desired.

**VARIATIONS:**
1. Place a leaf on a box lid and cover entire lid with foil. Press and rub foil until leaf print shows through, and leave as a permanent decoration for the box lid.
2. Cover other objects with foil, such as yarn glued to cardboard, scraps of heavy paper glued to cardboard, or items such as buttons. Press and rub foil over the objects.
3. Paint any of the above foiled projects with black paint, and then rub paint off before completely dry. Gives an antique look.

# MUSHROOM SPORE PRINT

**MATERIALS:**
gilled mushroom
dark construction paper
bowl
hairspray, optional

**PROCESS:**
1. Collect a fresh gilled mushroom (like the kind you see in the grocery stores).
2. Remove stem.
3. Place mushroom flat side down on dark paper.
4. Cover the mushroom cap with a bowl to prevent drafts from blowing the spores away.
5. Let sit for four hours or so.
6. Carefully lift the cap and see the print the spores have made.
7. Spray print with hairspray to prevent smudging print, optional.
8. Wash hands when finished making spore prints.

**VARIATIONS:**
1. Frame spore print and hang.
2. Make a collection of different prints from different mushrooms.

## MATERIALS:

4 eggs
2 cups of sugar
4 cups of all purpose flour
1 teaspoon of baking powder
1 teaspoon of salt
anise seeds, optional

flour
plate
rolling pin
mixing bowl
rotary or electric mixer
knife
spatula

items to press into cookie dough such as:
nuts and bolts
small toy trucks
plastic baby doll feet
blocks
forks
rubber stamps (clean)
plastic letters

## PROCESS:

1. Beat eggs in mixing bowl with mixer until eggs are light and fluffy (5 or 6 minutes). Continue to beat mixture and add sugar slowly, beating for 10 to 12 minutes. (The mixture will be thick and pale yellow.)

2. Mix the flour with baking powder and salt, and add to the egg-sugar mixture. Hand mix until mixture forms a dough.

3. Turn out about 1/2 or 1/3 of the dough onto lightly floured surface. Roll out the dough with rolling pin to about 1/3" thickness. Add a little flour to the dough if it is too sticky.

4. Dust *clean* nuts, bolts, plastic letters, or other items with flour. Press into dough and remove.

5. Use knife to cut pressed dough into cookie shapes. Then lift shapes carefully with a spatula, and place on plate.

6. Allow cookies to dry overnight uncovered.

7. Preheat oven to 300°. Grease cookie sheets. Sprinkle sheets with anise seeds, if desired.

8. Place pressed cookies on sheets and bake for 15 or 16 minutes or until cookies are completely baked and dry.

## VARIATIONS:

1. Try food pressing on gingerbread dough, liver paté, braunschweiger, ice cream, or fresh sandwich bread.

2. Experiment with cookie cutters used with the pressing steps.

# WEAVING AND CRAFTS

chapter 4

# BRANCH WEAVING

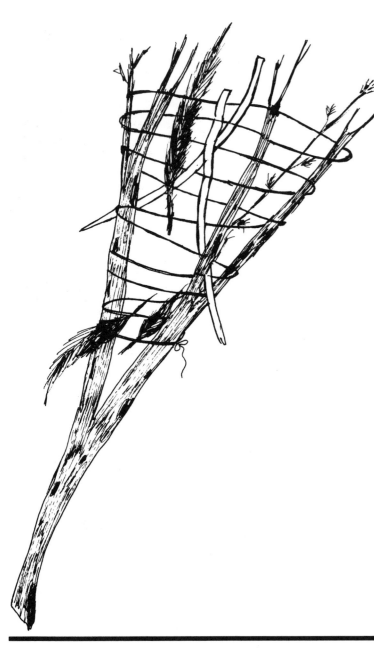

**MATERIALS:**
branch, with at least three smaller branches
colored yarn, about 2 yards each
nature items:
 long grasses
 cattail fluff and leaves
 feathers
 corn husks
 leather strips

**PROCESS:**
1.  Starting at bottom of small branch, loop yarn around and around, continuing to loop out towards end of branch.
2.  Weave yarn, grasses, leaves, and other nature items through first wool loops. Weaving may be random or a planned design.
3.  Hang branch, stick in can of sand, or display on table or shelf.

**VARIATIONS:**
1.  Add strips of cloth or paper.
2.  Thread used beads and jewelry on yarn before weaving.
3.  Tie shells, seed pods, colored macaroni, or other items on yarn before weaving.

**Suggestion:**
These materials may be used over and over again by unwrapping branch weaving and doing again, or using for other projects.

# FENCE WEAVING

## MATERIALS:
fence (chain-link or any other variety)
strips of burlap
strips of fabric
grasses
cattail leaves
reeds
ropes
string
yarn

## PROCESS:
1. Think of the fence as a loom.
2. Begin weaving materials such as strips of fabric or grasses and leaves through the fence.
3. Include some additional items that birds might enjoy, such as seeds, nuts, or little net bags of suet.
4. Remove weaving at end of day if you are concerned about rain.
5. For a more permanent weaving, omit any fabrics or papers that would disintegrate. Leave up as long as desired, but remember to take down at some point when the weather has worked its power on the beauty.

## VARIATIONS:
1. Weave a swing-set or monkey climber.
2. Pull ropes from the top of a pole or fence post out in a tent fashion. Weave through the ropes.
3. Try making a May-pole.
4. Design a loom outdoors by tacking or nailing string to a fence. Weave through the string.

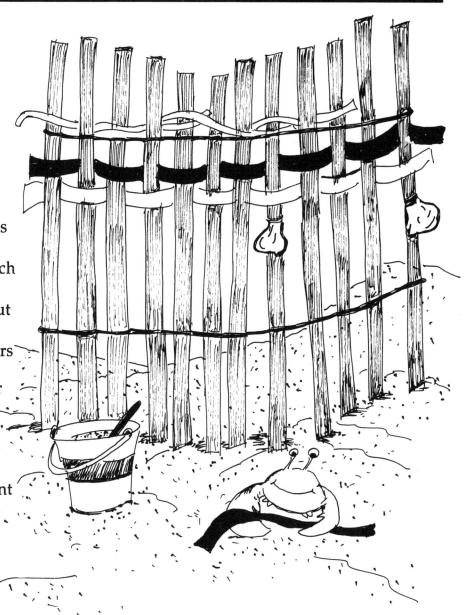

# WEAVING TRAYS

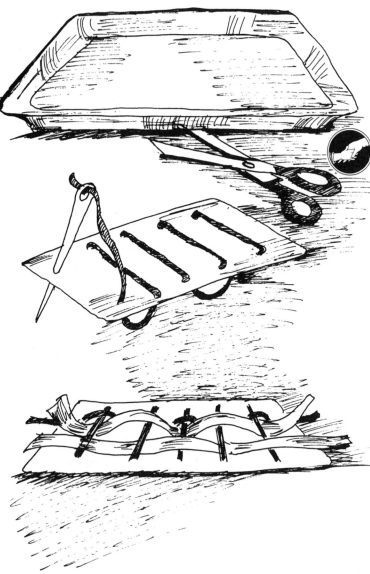

**MATERIALS:**
styrofoam meat trays, used and washed
scissors
yarn, threaded on plastic darning needle
yarn, ribbon, long reeds or grasses

**PROCESS:**
1. Cut a rectangle or square from center of meat tray.
   (Hint: Save scrap for other projects such as printing.)
2. Thread needle with yarn, and tie knot in end of yarn.
3. Begin wrapping back and forth, back and forth across tray forming the strands to be used for weaving called the "warp".
4. Tie, knot, or tape when complete and ready for weaving.
5. Weave ribbon or yarn back and forth through warp. Use a planned pattern or a random pattern.
   (Hint: To secure weaving while working, tape, staple, or sew yarn into meat tray at each end.)
6. Shells, beads, or macaroni can be added during weaving. Long reeds or grasses may also be added or used in place of ribbon or yarn.

**VARIATIONS:**
1. Any object with a hole in it can be used for threading: cereals, pastas, spools, buttons, or papers with holes punched are great.
2. Remove weavings from meat trays and use as placemats, pot holders, or hangings.
3. Try the same weaving approach on loosely woven burlap or netting scraps. Tape or tack fabric to a simple wooden frame first.

# FRUIT BASKET WEAVING

**MATERIALS:**
fruit basket, plastic
assorted yarn colors
ribbons
grasses or reeds
masking tape

**PROCESS:**
1. Tape end of yarn to make a "needle".
2. Weave yarn in and out of the holes in the basket.
3. Add other decorative items such as ribbon, grasses, or reeds.
4. Use basket as a decorative container or gift.

**VARIATIONS:**
1. Wind yarn around basket and then weave through the yarn.
2. Soak woven basket in starch or thinned white glue for a permanent, crisp result.
3. Fill basket with treasures and give to someone special.

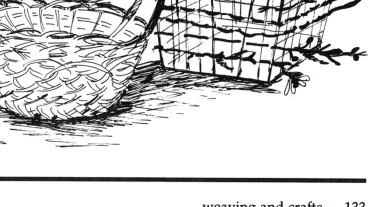

# SIX PACK RING WEAVING

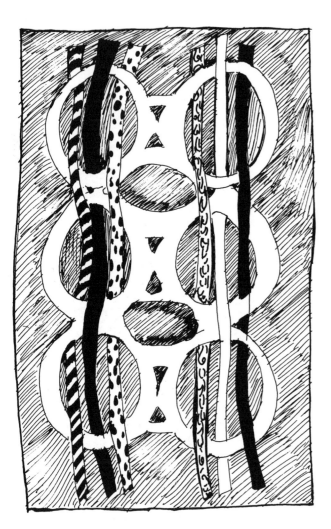

**MATERIALS:**
plastic six pack rings
paper
poster board or tag
scissors
stapler
staples

**PROCESS:**
1. Cut paper into strips.
2. Starting on the short side of the six pack rings, slide strip through rings going *under* one ring, *over* the next, and *under* again.
3. Slide another strip next to the first one. This time go *over* one ring and *under* the next, then *over* again.
4. Place other strips over and under the rings. Feel free to weave a random or planned design.
5. Repeat the weaving process until the six pack ring is filled.
6. Staple weaving onto a poster board or tag background and display.

**VARIATIONS:**
1. Weave yarn, feathers, straws, or other items.
2. Join six pack weavings to form a large weaving. Use string, tape, yarn, or stapler to join.

# SHRINKERS

## MATERIALS:
plastic lids or salad bar plastic containers
permanent marking pens
hole punch
yarn or paper clip

cookie sheet
aluminum foil
spatula
275° oven

## PROCESS:
1. Preheat oven to 275°.
2. Pre-cut plastic shapes or draw directly on uncut plastic. Uncut designs will curl and be unusual and lumpy. Cut plastic will lay flatter.
3. Punch two holes touching each other to make one large hole in each shape.
4. Color with pens on plastic.
5. Place plastic on foil-covered cookie sheet. Then place in oven. (Hint: If plastic curls too much, use a cooler oven.)
6. When plastic is shrunken, flat, and thick, remove from oven and press with spatula.
7. Cool.
8. Insert yarn or paper clip for hanging.

## VARIATIONS:
1. Before shrinking, outline edge of drawing with felt pen for a framed look.
2. Make a charm bracelet with many designs attached.
3. Good for holiday ornaments.

## WARNING:
Work in a well-ventilated area.

*When consulted about possible dangers involving gases from this project, environmental authorities advised that merely melting the plastic and thereby shrinking it was not harmful. However, burning the plastic or styrofoam releases gases into the atmosphere which are harmful to the ozone layer. Recycling this project as art is a good use for left over styrofoam and plastic as long as the products are not burned.*

# SHRINKLES I

**MATERIALS:**
styrofoam meat trays, used and clean
felt pens (permanent work best)
scissors
white glue
spatula or craft stick
baking sheet
aluminum foil
300° oven

**PROCESS:**
1. Draw a picture on a styrofoam meat tray with markers.
2. Place on baking sheet covered with aluminum foil.
3. Poke hole for hanging before baking.
4. Bake at 300° for 3 - 5 minutes. If design curls, press flat with spatula or stick. (Adult supervision suggested.)
5. Hang with yarn, rubber band, or wire.

**VARIATIONS:**
1. Cut out pre-colored shape, punch hole, and bake.
2. Use for a pendant or ornament.
3. Glue magnet to back of design and use for refrigerator magnet.
4. Glue jewelry clasp to back and wear as pin.

**CAUTION:**
Bake in well-ventilated area.

*When consulted about possible dangers involving gases from this project, environmental authorities advised that merely melting the plastic and thereby shrinking it was not harmful. However, burning the plastic or styrofoam releases gases into the atmosphere which are harmful to the ozone layer. Recycling this project as art is a good use for left over styrofoam and plastic as long as the products are not burned.*

# SHRINKLES II

**MATERIALS:**
plastic beverage cups
yarn or thin wire
scissors or hole puncher
baking sheet (metal)
350° oven
pulverized crayons or crayon shavings

**PROCESS:**
1. Punch or cut hole in cups with scissors or hole puncher.
2. Place plastic beverage cups right side up on baking sheet, not touching each other.
3. Fill each cup with one inch of crushed crayons or crayon shavings.
4. Bake at 350° for 1 to 2 minutes or until plastic cups melt. (Adult help suggested.)
5. Remove from oven and cool.
6. Hang with yarn or wire attached securely.

**VARIATIONS:**
1. After baking, glue clasp to back side and wear as a pin, or attach elastic band and use as hair ornament.
2. After baking, glue magnet to back and use for refrigerator magnet.
3. Use as a Christmas tree ornament.
4. Use scissors to make various snips and cuts in cups prior to baking.
5. Paint with acrylic paints, and add glitter when cool.

**CAUTION:**
Bake in well-ventilated area.

*When consulted about possible dangers involving gases from this project, environmental authorities advised that merely melting the plastic and thereby shrinking it was not harmful. However, burning the plastic or styrofoam releases gases into the atmosphere which are harmful to the ozone layer. this project as art is a good use for left over styrofoam and plastic as long as the products are not burned.*

# PAPERWEIGHT JARS

**MATERIALS:**
small glass jar with lid
collected items such as:
    seashells
    pieces of colored glass
    pebbles
    gravel
    coral

**PROCESS:**
1. Make sure that your collected items are clean and dry.
2. Place collected items in glass jar and fill with water.
3. Secure the lid onto your jar and turn it upside down.
4. Display your glass paperweight on a desk or windowsill.

**VARIATIONS:**
1. Use water colored with food coloring.
2. Add glitter or tiny bits of styrofoam for a "snow jar".

# TIN CAN PENCIL HOLDER

## MATERIALS:

empty tin can or frozen juice can
white glue or craft glue
paper, paper bags, or newspaper
scissors

pencils
masking tape or cellophane tape
markers, glitter, beads, sequins (optional)
sunflower or pumpkin seeds (optional)

## PROCESS:

1. Make sure can is clean and dry.
2. Cut paper long enough to fit around the can.
3. Lay the can on the paper so that the open side touches the top edge of the paper.
4. Wrap the paper around the can and tape it temporarily with a single piece of tape.
5. Push paper down and around the bottom of the can to form a crease. (This measures the paper to fit.)
6. Unfasten the tape and open up paper.
7. Cut with scissors along crease.
8. Wrap the paper around the can and tape securely.
9. Decorate pencil holder with cut paper designs, sequins, glitter, markers, sunflower seeds, pumpkin seeds, sponge prints, or other decorations.

## VARIATIONS:

1. Use an empty cardboard canister such as oatmeal, potato chip, or cornmeal instead of can.
2. Try decorating by sticking bits of paper or confetti to a measured piece of clear contact paper. Stick to can.

# STAINED GLASS LANTERN

**MATERIALS:**
glass jar
white glue
water
paintbrush
container
tissue wrapping paper or craft tissue paper
scissors
small votive candle

**PROCESS:**
1. Peel label from glass jar. Wash and dry.
2. Pour some glue into a container and add some water. Stir until the solution is like milk.
3. Tear or cut small pieces of tissue paper and brush on jar with glue solution. Brush the solution under and over each piece of tissue paper.
4. Let dry.
5. Add a votive candle and light it with an adult to help. (CAUTION)
6. Enjoy the colorful stained glass lantern.

**VARIATIONS:**
1. Use liquid starch instead of glue. Do not thin.
2. Cover rocks, wood, cardboard, paper plates, or cans (painted white first) with tissue and glue.

# SOUP CAN LANTERN

**MATERIALS:**
cans, washed and dried
hammer
nails, various sizes
water and freezer
candle, optional

**PROCESS:**
1. Fill can with water and freeze until solid (2 days works well).
2. Draw design on can, if desired, or work free hand. (Hint: Try your name, a picture, or a seasonal or theme idea.)
3. Put frozen can on pillow or towel while working.
4. Use any size nails to make holes by hammering on design.
5. Insert thin wire or coat hanger through holes for hanging.
6. Insert candle and light up the night. (CAUTION)

**VARIATIONS:**
1. Use for outdoor party table decoration.
2. Use for holiday decoration.
3. Try snipping edges with tin ships, but use caution. Sharp! (CAUTION)
4. After punching design, snip a 2″ piece from the side of a tuna can. Place over bulb in standard outlet variety night light.

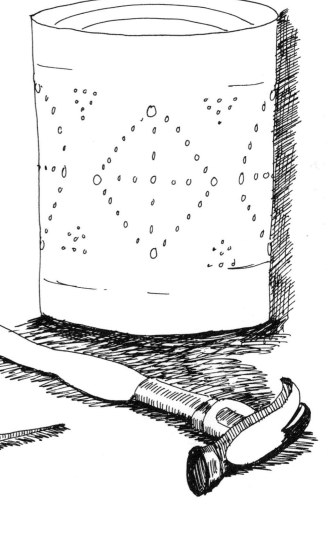

# LUMINARIES

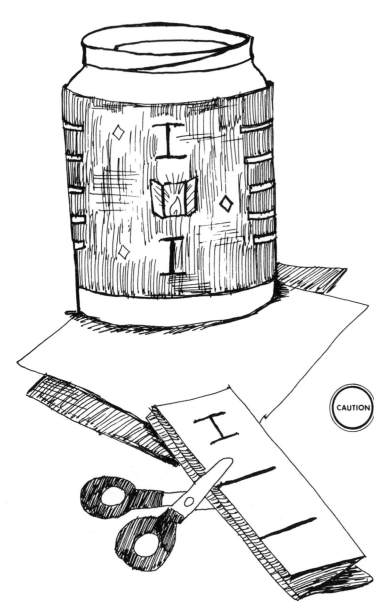

**MATERIALS:**

| | |
|---|---|
| heavy paper | tape |
| art tissue, any color — one sheet | jar |
| scissors | candle |
| ruler | sand |

**PROCESS:**

1. Cut a heavy piece of paper to fit all the way around a mayonnaise or peanut butter jar, forming a cylinder which is as tall as the jar.
2. Cut little holes and designs into the heavy paper. (Note: Any creative design works well, or make little foldback shutters or an accordion cut. See illustrations.)
3. When cuts are complete, glue a sheet of tissue to the back of the heavy paper. Trim away extra, saving pieces for future projects such as Lentil-piece, page 164.
4. Wrap the heavy paper with tissue around the jar. Tape or glue to hold.
5. Put sand in the jar to keep it from tipping easily.

CAUTION

6. Add a candle.
7. Light with adult supervision. (Use a long piece of spaghetti and light it like a match. Then reach way down inside the jar and light candle.)

**VARIATIONS:**

1. Instead of using the above tissue ideas, simply glue tissue to the outside of the jar. Then add the design-cut paper in a cylinder around the decorated jar.
2. Use Luminaries to brighten a table, a stairway, or a garden path.

# MASKING TAPE VASE

**MATERIALS:**
masking tape
shoe polish with a sponge tip applicator
glass bottle, jar, or tin can

**PROCESS:**
1. Tear off small portions of tape and press to outside of bottle, jar, or can. Cover completely, overlapping edges of tape.
2. Stain the masking tape with shoe polish.
3. Let dry.
4. Fill with flowers or favorite things.

**VARIATIONS:**
1. Use watered, thin acrylic paints and a sponge instead of shoe polish.
2. Rub tape with instant coffee on a wet rag for a leather look.
3. Rub tape with rag dipped in Kool-Aid which has been moistened with a little water. Bright color!

# WEB ART

## MATERIALS:
spider web
black paper
talcum powder
pump hairspray, optional

## PROCESS:
1. Hunt spider webs on a calm day. (Look for webs that are no longer inhabited.)
2. Sprinkle powder on web.
3. Carefully lift web with paper until web breaks free and is stuck to paper.
4. Spray with pump hairspray.

## VARIATIONS:
1. Spray paper with hairspray. Work quickly, following the same powder and paper technique above.
2. Sit beside an inhabited web and draw the same design you see.
3. Glue string or thread on black paper in a web design.

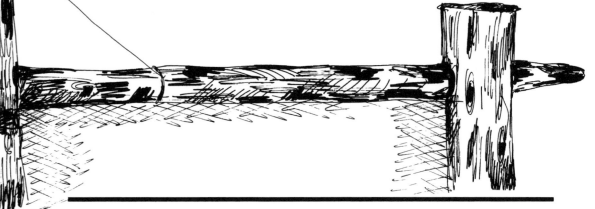

# LEAF SKELETONS

**MATERIALS:**
8"x10" piece of wood
carpet scrap
tacks or nails
shoebrush or hairbrush with animal bristles
leaf
plastic wrap
newspaper
iron

**PROCESS:**
1. Tack a scrap of carpet to the piece of wood.
2. Put a leaf on the carpet, top side up.
3. Hold leaf with one hand, and tap the leaf gently with the bristle end of the brush held with the other hand. Do this until the fleshy parts of the leaf are worn away.
4. Turn the leaf over now and then, and tap the other side.
5. When complete, only the lacey skeleton of the leaf will be left.
6. To save and enjoy, place the skeleton between two sheets of plastic wrap, covered with a sheet of newspaper.
7. Using a warm iron, press the plastic coated leaf quickly, and the plastic will melt and stick to the leaf.

**VARIATIONS:**
1. Put skeleton between two sheets of clear contact paper.
2. Put skeleton between two sheets of waxed paper and iron as you did the plastic wrap.
3. Glue the leaf skeleton to paper with glue. Cover or frame.

# CATTAIL FLUFF PILLOW

**MATERIALS:**
cattail fluff, late November or early December
two pieces of fabric the same size
needle and thread

**PROCESS:**
1. Collect cattail fluff in early winter around ponds and swampy areas. Wear boots.
2. Place two pieces of fabric together. Sew around all sides to make a small pillow, leaving a hand-sized opening at one end.
3. Turn fabric so sewing is inside.
4. Stuff pillow with cattail fluff.
5. Stitch remaining opening with needle and thread.

**VARIATIONS:**
1. While collecting fluff, collect leaves to use for weaving baskets and mats or other weaving projects.
2. Sew pillow with sewing machine to save time.
3. Decorate fabric before sewing with any variety of ideas such as:
   fabric crayons
   embroidery
   stenciled finger prints
4. Use old T-shirt, jeans, scarves, or other clothing for the fabric. Or use an old sheet, pillow case, or tablecloth.

# SUNFLOWER SEED WREATH

**MATERIALS:**
mature sunflower head
wheat, millet, and pecans
wire
knife or scissors

**PROCESS:**
1. Remove sunflower blossom from stalk.
2. Cut center from seed head to form a wreath. Save center for Plastic Bird Feeder, page 166.
3. Dry seed wreath for several days.
4. Wire decorations to top of wreath such as millet, wheat, and pecans. Any bird favorites will do.
5. Hang on tree or fence for birds to eat, or give as a gift to a bird lover.

**VARIATIONS:**
1. Other animals love Sunflower Seed Wreaths, too. Let your hamster, gerbil, mouse, or rat have a nibble.
2. Hang Sunflower Seed Wreath low to the ground outdoors for a nocturnal creature's snack.

# GRAPE VINE WREATH

**MATERIALS:**
wild grape vines
heavy scissors
ribbons, if desired
string or wire

**PROCESS:**
**In the Fall, gather wild grape vines in wooded areas or gardens. They often grow in a tangle on trees and small shrubs. They are tough and wooden, and in the spring they have fruit.**

1. Gather wild grape vines.
   (Hint: A pair of heavy scissors or cutters may be needed.)
2. Bend the gathered grape vines into a circle.
3. Twist more grape vines together into the circle.
4. Tie ribbons on your wreath to decorate.
5. Tie a wire or string to display.

**VARIATIONS:**
1. Use the grape vines to create other shapes.
2. Decorate wreath or other shapes with pinecones, grasses, flowers, or other items you have gathered.

# PINE BRANCH WREATH

**MATERIALS:**
fresh pine branches
heavy scissors
metal coat hanger
ribbon, if desired

**PROCESS:**
1. Bend metal coat hanger to form a circle.
   (Hint: Leave the hook on top of the circle.)
2. Twist pine branches around the metal coat hanger.
   (Hint: Use scissors to trim the pine branches if they are too long and awkward to work with.)
3. Continue twisting pine branches around the metal coat hanger until the wreath looks nice and full.
4. Tie a bright ribbon on the wreath to decorate.
5. Hang the wreath up using the hook on top.

**VARIATIONS:**
1. Attach any greens to wire circle, such as juniper, cedar, fir, or spruce.
2. Try using wire or string to attach greens.
3. Try making a wreath of dried grasses, weeds, or flowers.

# NATURE WREATH

**MATERIALS:**

| | |
|---|---|
| 2 sheets heavy cardboard | seeds |
| scissors | dried leaves |
| string | ribbon |
| pine cones | pencil |
| nuts | large plate |
| seed pods | smaller plate |

**PROCESS:**

1. Cut cardboard into a wreath shape by tracing plates. Glue two wreath shapes together for extra strength. Wreath will be double thicknesses of cardboard.

2. Punch a small hole with scissors for hanging.

3. Glue nature items to the cardboard. Use plenty of glue. (Older children may use a glue gun with adult assistance.)

4. Fill wreath shapes completely with nature items. Add other objects, scraps, and decorations if you like.

5. Allow wreath to dry overnight.

**VARIATIONS:**

1. Paint wreath with white glue or clear gloss enamel.

2. Use nuts, bolts, nails, screws and other hardware items for a fun wreath.

3. Use wreath flat on table for a center piece. Add a candle in the center, if you like.

# TRIM A TREE FOR BIRDS

**MATERIALS:**
stale bread
cookie cutters, knife, or scissors
peanut butter
yarn
pretzels, donuts
orange halves, scooped out
suet and seed

**PROCESS:**
**Make a festive gift for the birds:**
1. Begin by cutting stale bread into pretty shapes with scissors, cookie cutter, or a knife.
2. Spread bread with peanut butter. (Then press this into a tray of bird seed, if you like.)
3. Hang the edible ornaments from a tree outside with yarn (which birds will use for nests later).

**Add other treats, too:**
4. Scoop out an orange half, fill with suet and seed, and place in crook of a tree branch.
5. Hang stale donuts or pretzels from branches.
6. Watch from your window and enjoy the feeling of giving.

**VARIATIONS:**
1. Fill a net bag with "bird-pudding" and hang from tree: mixture of suet or vegetable shortening, peanut butter, eggs, seeds, bread, left over meats, or any other thing birds enjoy.
2. Fill a piece of netting with dryer lint for nesting materials.

# HOLIDAY CHAIN

**MATERIALS:**
popcorn or styrofoam peanuts
cranberries (whole fresh)
needle
thread
scissors

**PROCESS:**
1. Pop the popcorn and leave uncovered until stale.
2. Push thread through the eye of needle and *leave the end on spool.*

(CAUTION)

3. Push the threaded needle through a single popcorn or cranberry and slide it to the spool. (Be careful not to poke fingers with the needle.)
4. Repeat this process until you have a long string of cranberries or popcorn.
5. Cut the spool of thread from the end of the popcorn or cranberry string, and tie a knot at both ends.
6. String your popcorn or cranberry chain around a tree or plant, indoors or out. Birds will enjoy this gift, too.

**VARIATIONS:**
1. Use holly berry or dogwood berries for a brightly colored chain.
2. Make beads from clay (see Index under "Clay"), being sure to poke a hole in each bead before drying. Use as berries to string.
3. Save beads from old jewelry and string with popcorn or cranberries.

# VEGGIE GARLAND

**MATERIALS:**
large carrots
potato peeler
knife
string
needle
newsprint

**PROCESS:**
1. Peel the carrot with the potato peeler.
2. Cut the carrot into slices.
3. Thread the needle with string. **CAUTION**
   (Hint: A needle with a large eye works best.)
4. Thread carrot slices, leaving spaces between them.
   (Note: Tying knots between or adding other bits of
   decorations, such as old beads or macaroni, is effective.)
5. Keep stringing until you have a garland the length you
   like.
6. Lay the garland on newsprint to dry for about 10 days.
7. Drape, wrap, or hang to decorate as you please.

**VARIATIONS:**
1. Make a short garland and wear as a necklace.
2. Use dried carrot slices as part of sculptures or mobiles.
3. Decorate a tree outdoors with carrot garlands for the birds
   and animals. They will use the string when the carrots are
   gone.

# WILDFLOWER CHAIN

**MATERIALS:**
wildflowers such as:
    daisies
    Queen Anne's lace
    black-eyed Susan
    violets
    dandelions

**PROCESS:**
1. Remove the leaves from wildflowers.
2. Tie wildflowers together by the stems.
3. Make a necklace, bracelet, chain, belt, or head garland. (Hint: Remember to make necklace big enough to slip over your head.)

**VARIATIONS:**
1. Dry and press wildflowers for other projects. (See Index under "Wildflowers".)
2. Tie flowers to a tree or bush outside.

# FEATHER NECKLACE

**MATERIALS:**
feathers
heavy string, twine, leather strips, or leather shoe strings
thin wire
scissors

**PROCESS:**
1. Gather feathers at the beach, park, or woods.
2. Twist wire around the bottom of a feather quill.
3. Twist wire around feather quills until you have enough to make a necklace.
4. Twist completed feathers onto heavy string to make a feather necklace!

**VARIATIONS:**
1. Try making a feather bracelet.
2. Try making a feather pendant using a diaper pin or safety pin.
3. Use feathers in weavings, collages, bark baskets. (See Index under "Feathers".)

# PEBBLE NECKLACE

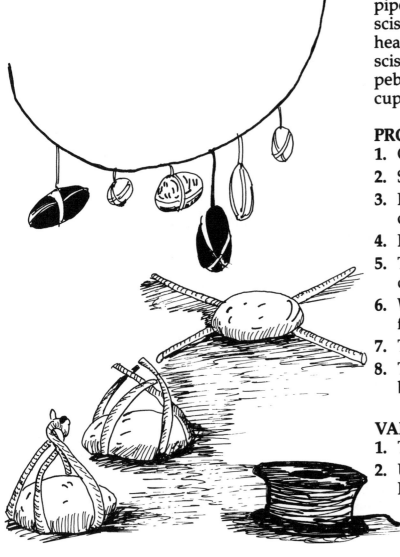

**MATERIALS:**
pipe cleaners or thin wire
scissors to cut wire
heavy string, twine or leather strips
scissors
pebbles
cups or bowls

**PROCESS:**
1. Gather pebbles.
2. Separate into bowls or cups.
3. Place two pipe cleaners on a flat surface, one on top of the other in the shape of an "X".
4. Place the pebble in the center of the "X".
5. Twist the pipe cleaners around the pebble so that it doesn't move around.
6. Wrap each piece in the same way until there are enough for a necklace.
7. Twist each wrapped pebble on string, twine or leather.
8. Tie the string of nature pieces into a loop and wear the beautiful pebble necklace!

**VARIATIONS:**
1. Try using nuts or seashells instead of pebbles.
2. Use pebbles for a variety of projects. See "Pebbles" in Index.

# SEED NECKLACE

**MATERIALS:**
pumpkin, sunflower, squash, or other seeds
needle
spool or thread
scissors
thimble

**PROCESS:**
1. Make sure that your seeds are clean and dry.
2. Cut a long piece of thread from the spool.
3. Thread the needle.
4. Tie a knot at the end.
5. Using the thimble, push the needle through each seed one at a time, and push the seeds all the way to the end of the thread.
6. Fill the whole thread with seeds.

**VARIATIONS:**
1. Try for a pattern of seeds.
2. Add beads from broken jewelry for decoration.

# NEWSPAPER BEADS

**MATERIALS:**

sheets of newspaper or magazine    yardstick
toothpicks    pencil
glue    darning needle
scissors    nylon thread or cord

**PROCESS:**

1. Mark off 1" intervals all the way down the left side of the newspaper page with the yardstick.
2. Now mark the other side, beginning ½" from the top. Then continue to mark 1" intervals on this side, all the way down the page.
3. Connect each left hand mark with two opposite ones with yardstick to make triangles (see illustration).
4. Cut out the triangles.
5. Place a toothpick across the wide end, and wind the paper 2 or 3 times tightly onto the toothpick.
6. Hold the paper in place and glue inside strip. Wind up until point is securely glued.
7. Remove toothpick and let bead dry.
8. Make about 10 beads.
9. Thread beads onto a piece of nylon thread or cord. Tie ends.
10. Wear as a necklace.

**VARIATIONS:**

1. Alternate newspaper beads with wooden beads or beads saved from broken jewelry.
2. Experiment with papers to make beads, colorful comic strips being particularly pretty.

# WALNUT SHELL BOATS

**MATERIALS:**

nut cracker
walnuts
soft bubble gum or beeswax
toothpicks

paper
crayons, markers, or pencils
scissors

**PROCESS:**

1. Adult: crack open the walnut so that there are two halves.
2. Remove the nut inside the shell.
   (Hint: Yummy!)
3. Fill walnut shell with soft bubble gum or beeswax.
4. Cut a sail from the paper and decorate it with crayons, pencils, or markers.
5. Insert a toothpick through the bottom part of the sail, then bend the sail slightly and push the toothpick through the top of the sail (or glue a triangle to the toothpick).
6. Insert the completed sail into the bubble gum or beeswax.
7. Sail the walnut shell boat in the sink or bucket of water, down a creek, or in a puddle.

**VARIATIONS:**
**Walnut shells can also be:**
   tiny mouse cradle
   penguin
   diorama miniatures
   hat for a doll
   dishes, tea sets
   anything imaginable

# EGG SHELL PLANTERS

**MATERIALS:**
egg shells (broken into halves)
egg carton
potting soil or dirt
seeds
water
spoon

**PROCESS:**
1. Place halved egg shells in egg carton, one egg shell per cup.
2. Spoon some potting soil or dirt into each egg shell.
3. Place a seed into each egg shell and cover with soil.
4. Place egg carton with egg shells in a sunny place.
5. Water egg shells gently each day and watch seedlings sprout.

**VARIATIONS:**
1. Dye halved egg shells in a mixture of food coloring, water, and a bit of white vinegar. When dry, use as planters.
2. Dye eggs in Natural Berry Dye (page 196) or Onion Skin Dye (page 201) before breaking in half for planters.
3. See Eggheads (page 161).

# EGGHEADS

**MATERIALS:**
hard boiled egg
alfalfa seed
cotton balls
colored felt pens

**PROCESS:**
1. Carefully draw a face on an egg.
2. Cut off top of egg.
3. Remove egg from shell.
4. Fill empty shell with cotton balls.
5. Sprinkle seed on cotton.
6. Cover with small moistened cotton ball.
7. Set in window.
8. Seeds should sprout in a day and grow for 3 or 4 days.
9. Moisten cotton daily.
10. Remove top layer when sprouts have grown to allow the Egghead "hair" to stand up straight.

**VARIATIONS:**
1. Paint a family of faces on several eggs.
2. Decorate eggs in designs instead of faces.
3. Make eggs creatures or silly critters.

# WOOD CHIP GARDEN

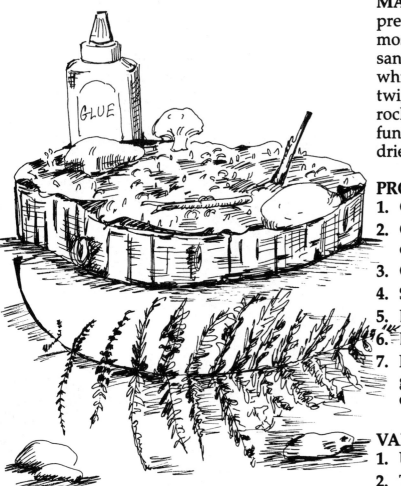

**MATERIALS:**
pre-cut slices of logs or sticks
moss
sand
white glue
twigs
rocks
fungi
dried weeds

**PROCESS:**
1. Collect a log slice of about 1 inch thick and 4 inches across.
2. Collect moss, lichens, river sand, assorted rocks, twigs, and other things to decorate a garden.
3. Cover wooden disc with white glue.
4. Sprinkle sand on glue, shaking off the excess.
5. Begin gluing other items to design the landscape.
6. Dry.
7. In a few days, spray with water to moisten moss. The garden will stay green and grow if moistened and kept out of the sunlight.

**VARIATIONS:**
1. Use a larger slab of wood and larger plants.
2. Try peeling bark off a fallen tree and build a garden on bark. (Birch works well.)

# PINE CONE GARDEN

**MATERIALS:**
pine cones
grass seed
small flower seeds
nail
circular scrap of wood
saucer

**PROCESS:**
1. Nail a big, loosely-shaped pine cone to a circular scrap of wood. One nail will do.
2. Set the pine cone and wood in a saucer of water.
3. Plant grass and small flower seeds between the pine cone's sections. No soil is necessary.
4. Keep saucer filled with water.
5. Watch for sprouting seeds and a little pine cone garden.

**VARIATIONS:**
1. Nail a pine cone to a scrap of wood. Cut out the top of the pine cone. Drip some warm wax into the cone and then insert the candle. It will adhere to the warm wax.
2. Cover a pine cone with glue, roll in ordinary salt, and use to burn in a fireplace. The salt gives off a bright, yellow flame. Try other ingredients such as:
   copper nitrate — green
   copper sulfate — blue
   calcium chloride — orange
   potassium chloride — violet
      (Available at drug stores.)

# LENTIL-PIECE

**MATERIALS:**
cotton (not polyester) batting
dinner plate
1 cup lentils, sproutable (from health food store)
candle (broad based)

**PROCESS:**
1. Set a candle in the middle of a plate.
2. Line the plate with cotton, a single layer.
3. Dampen cotton. Then cover with a layer of lentils.
4. Mist the lentils. Pour off any standing water.
5. To speed germination, cover the plate with plastic wrap.
6. Put in a window sill, avoiding direct sun.
7. To maintain, check moisture of cotton every other day, adding a few drops of water if necessary. After a week's growth, remove the plastic and mist plants daily.

**VARIATIONS:**
1. Sow this wreath of sprouts early in December, and by Christmas Eve the wreath should be full and green. Harvest sprouts for salad.
2. Try this wreath with any sproutable seed or grain such as oats, wheat, or chives.
3. Instead of a wax candle, decorate a mayonnaise or peanut butter jar with tissue glued on with thinned white glue. Put a votive candle in the jar for a lantern effect.
4. Cover a jar with any decorations and place a votive candle in the jar as a lantern.

# MILK CARTON PLANTER

**MATERIALS:**
paper milk or juice carton
scissors
white glue
paper
pencils, markers, or crayons
earth or potting soil
seedling

**PROCESS:**
1. Cut off the top of the milk or juice carton.
2. Glue paper to all sides of carton to cover writing.
3. Decorate paper with crayons, markers, or pencils.
4. Fill with potting soil or earth, and add a seedling.
5. Place in a sunny spot and water as needed.

**VARIATIONS:**
1. Plant a seed in your planter and water. Watch it grow.
2. Try planting vegetable starts such as beans or corn and transplant outdoors when ready.

# PLASTIC BIRD FEEDER

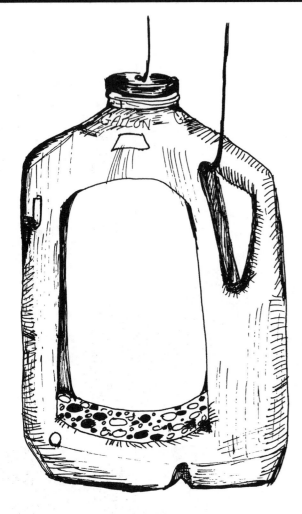

**MATERIALS:**
plastic gallon milk container
heavy scissors
wire or string
bird food such as seeds, bread, or dry cereal
white glue
wild flowers, grass, or small pebbles for decoration

**PROCESS:**
1. Cut through milk carton with heavy scissors.
2. Make several openings large enough for birds to enter and exit.
3. Leave about 2 inches of milk carton at the bottom so that you have a place to put the bird food.
4. Use the white glue, wild flowers, and pebbles to decorate the sides of your bird feeder.

**VARIATIONS:**
1. Fill with suet or peanut butter for bird food.
2. Fill with planting soil and seeds, and enjoy a hanging garden.

# PLASTIC BOTTLE TERRARIUM

**MATERIALS:**
two plastic bottles from pop or soda water
heavy scissors
soil
plants collected from outside

**PROCESS:**
1. Remove the heavy plastic bottom from one of the plastic bottles. Put aside.
2. Cut off the pouring spout top of the other plastic bottle.
3. Fill this plastic bottle with soil and plants which have been collected ahead of time.
4. Place the heavy plastic bottom that was put aside on top of the terrarium to make a lid.
5. Place the terrarium in a sunny spot and remember to water it as needed.

**VARIATIONS:**
1. Plant seeds in soil and grow plants or flowers.
2. Make paper plants and flowers for a permanent terrarium arrangement.

# GROCERY BASKETS

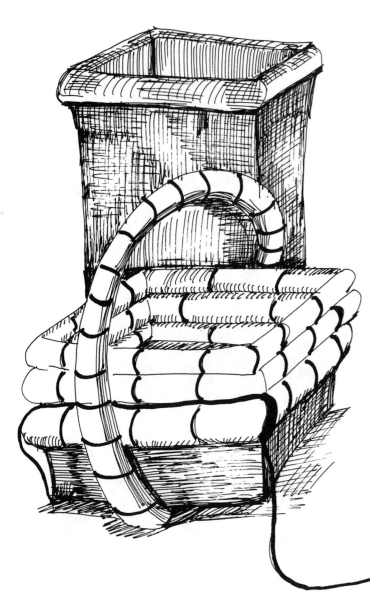

## MATERIALS:
four brown grocery bags
yarn
large darning needle

## PROCESS:
1. Roll rim of bag down to within 2 inches of its bottom.
2. Roll and insert second bag into first bag.
3. Roll and insert third bag into second bag, so there is a trio of stacked rolls.
4. For handle, cut bottom off fourth bag.
5. Roll sides down to make coil.
6. Slip handle over basket.
7. Loop yarn through bag layers to secure coils.
   (Note: Knot yarn at each ring, or continue strand from ring to ring. See illustration.)

## VARIATIONS:
**Use grocery baskets for:**
    holding presents
    homemade cookies
    homemade jams
    home grown house plant
    doll carry basket

# BARK BASKETS

## MATERIALS:
paper canister from powdered soft drink mix or oatmeal
white glue
heavy scissors
rubber bands
tree bark from a dead tree or log (remove bark in large sections)

## PROCESS:
1. Be sure that the tree bark is dry and free of dirt and insects.
2. Place canister inside the natural curve of the bark.
3. Trim top and bottom of bark to fit the length of the canister.
   (Hint: More than one piece of bark may be needed to fully cover the sides of the canister.)
4. Use white glue to attach bark to sides of canister. Hold in place with rubber bands.
5. Let dry.
6. Fill bark basket with your favorite things.

## VARIATIONS:
1. Use to display dried, gathered weeds and flowers.
2. Set a small potted plant inside container. It must have its own leak-proof pot.

# SQUASH-O-LANTERN

**MATERIALS:**
large squash such as acorn, butternut, or pumpkin
knife
marker
newspaper to spread over work surface
candle or flashlight

**PROCESS:**
**You probably already know how to make a Jack-o-lantern from a pumpkin. Did you know that you can also make a lantern from a squash?**
1. Draw a design or face on the shell of the squash or pumpkin.
2. Use a knife to carve along the lines.
3. Cut off the top of your squash or Jack-o-lantern and scoop out the inside so that only the shell remains.
4. If the squash does not have a flat bottom so that it can sit by itself, use a knife to cut off the bottom and make it even.
5. Use a flashlight or a candle to light up the squash-o-lantern or Jack-o-lantern.

**VARIATIONS:**
1. Paint on faces.
2. Glue on paper faces.

**NOTE:**
Some squashes are hard and are very difficult to carve. Microwave briefly to soften (prick shell with fork to vent.)

# GOURD ART

## MATERIALS:

large or small gourds (washed and dried)
knife
pencil
spoon
paints
newspaper
jar of water
rags
paintbrushes
markers

## PROCESS:

**Gourds can be made into many projects. Convert a gourd into a ladle, a birdfeeder, a jewelry box, a pencil holder, or use your own idea.**

1. Draw a line on the gourd as a guideline for cutting.

2. Use the knife to cut very lightly along the line.

3. Cut again along the same line deeply into the gourd. (Be very careful and go slowly.)

4. Scoop out all the insides with the spoon.

5. Let dry for one or two days.

6. Spread newspaper over a flat surface.

7. Place gourd on the newspaper.

8. Use the paintbrush, paints, and markers to decorate the outside of the gourd.

9. Use gourd for your own ideas.

## VARIATIONS:

1. Give the gourd as a gift filled with candy, toys, or small treasures such as shells or stones.

2. See Musical Gourd Shaker (page 172) and Gourd Guitar (page 173).

# MUSICAL GOURD SHAKER

**MATERIALS:**
crook neck gourd or other type of gourd
paper
scissors
masking tape, duct tape
small pebbles, seeds, or popcorn kernals
sharp knife
pencil
spoon
paints or markers (optional)

**PROCESS:**
1. Draw a circle onto the fullest part of the gourd with a pencil. (Hint: Soak in water overnight to soften shell.)
2. Use knife to first cut lightly over the pencil line and then cut again deeply into the gourd. (Adult help recommended.)
3. Lift off the outer layer of the gourd and scoop out the inside fleshy parts with a spoon.
4. Let the outer skin of the gourd dry.
5. Fill the gourd with small pebbles, seeds, or popcorn kernals.
6. Cover hole with large pieces of duct tape.
7. Use the Musical Gourd Shaker to create a rhythm, or accompany a favorite song.
8. Leave shaker plain or decorate with markers or paints.

**VARIATIONS:**
1. Decorate by scratching designs in gourd.
2. Fill gourd with used nuts, bolts, tiny car parts, and other metal pieces.

# GOURD GUITAR

**MATERIALS:**
crook neck or other type of gourd
rubber bands
sharp knife
pencil
spoon
paints or markers (optional)

**PROCESS:**
1. Draw a circle onto the fullest part of the gourd with a pencil.
   (Hint: Soften gourd's skin by soaking in water overnight.)
2. Use a sharp knife to first cut lightly on the pencil line and then cut deeply into the gourd. (Adult help recommended.)
3. Lift off the outer layer of the gourd and scoop out the inside fleshy parts of the gourd.
4. Let the remaining outer skin of the gourd dry.
5. Stretch rubber bands over the hole and strum the "guitar".
6. Leave guitar plain or add decorations with paints or markers.

**VARIATIONS:**
1. Designs may be scratched into gourd's skin as decoration.
2. Gourd may be covered with papier-maché and painted.

# ANIMAL TRACKS CASTING

**MATERIALS:**
plaster wall patch (available from lumber yard)
mixing container
water
large spoon
animal tracks such as:
   deer
   dog
   cat
   raccoon
   opossum
   lizard or
   people tracks

**PROCESS:**
1. Locate tracks. Look in wooded areas, along paths or in fields, along streams, lake or beach areas.
2. If tracks are dry, moisten the area with water carefully.
3. Mix plaster with water, according to package directions.
4. Pour or spoon plaster carefully into animal tracks.
5. Let dry for a day or until plaster is hard.
6. Remove plaster casting carefully from animal tracks.

**VARIATIONS:**
1. Preserve car, bike, or tire tracks.
2. Make tracks with hands, feet, or other tools and then preserve.
3. Make sasquatch or dinosaur tracks for fun.

# COLORFUL COAL CRYSTALS

**MATERIALS:**
charcoal briquettes
ammonia
iodized salt
liquid laundry bluing
throw-away aluminum pie tin
food coloring
measuring spoons
container

**PROCESS:**
1. In a container, mix together one or two tablespoons each of liquid bluing, iodized salt, and ammonia.
2. Place charcoal into a disposable container and add a few drops of food coloring into the pieces.
3. Pour solution over top of charcoal pieces.
4. Let stand until crystals form.
5. Replenish bluing, ammonia, and salt solution as it evaporates.
6. Enjoy the beautiful colors and shapes.

# KEEP CLAM

**MATERIALS:**
clam or oyster shells
hand drill (non electric)
modeling clay or moist clay
white glue
pieces of colorful fabric or felt
old beads, buttons, or jewelry
heavy yarn or string
scissors
thin scrap wire

**PROCESS:**
1. Make sure that your seashells are clean, dry and free of dirt and sand.
2. Place one half of your clam or oyster shell into a wad of modeling clay or moist clay so that it won't move.
3. Use a hand drill to slowly drill a hole through the top side of the clam or oyster shell.
4. Repeat drilling with other half of the clam or oyster shell.
5. Place a wire through the holes of both shells, and twist the wire together as a hinge.
6. Glue colorful fabric inside the shells.
7. Decorate the outside of the shell with yarns, beads, strings, colorful fabric, or other items. Glue as desired.
8. Place treasures inside the shell, when dry, and close tightly.

# FLOWER BOX PICTURES

**MATERIALS:**

cigar box or shallow cardboard box
dried flowers, weeds, grasses
stones
shells
figurines or small toys
twigs
lump of playdough or clay
scissors
paint
paper or fabric

**PROCESS:**

1. Cut away lid, if any.
2. Cover or paint box, if desired.
   (Note: Paint a scene in the box for a background, if you like.)
3. Put lumps of clay on the bottom of the space, pressing in firmly.
4. Stick stems of flowers, grasses, twigs, or other items into the clay.
5. Fix in a pretty or interesting arrangement.
6. Add stones, shells, and figurines, if you wish.

**VARIATIONS:**

1. Trim edge of box with scraps of rickrack, lace, or other fabric items with glue.
2. Design a landscape, fantasy land, Japanese garden, doll world, rainforest, or primeval forest.
3. Add twig animals.
4. Cover front of box with plastic wrap, if desired.

# CATTAIL BASKET

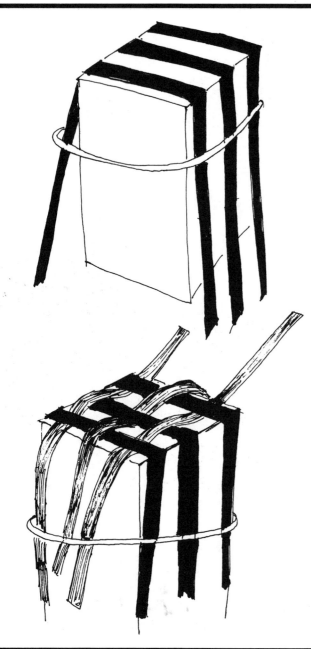

**MATERIALS:**

| | |
|---|---|
| newspaper | rubber bands |
| cattail leaves | sponge |

heavy scissors
tub or large container filled with water
shoe box with lid, or box about the size of a shoe box, stuffed
  with newspaper for strength

**PROCESS:**

1. Find fresh cattail leaves in swampy areas. Cut with heavy scissors close to the base.

2. Spread out fresh cattail leaves in a warm, dry area over newspaper to dry out until they become brownish-green in color (one to two weeks).

3. Soak dried cattail leaves in water for at least 15 minutes before using.

4. Stuff shoe box with newspaper and place lid on shoe box. Put a rubber band around the width of the shoe box.

5. Sit with the shoe box between your legs, rubber band side up.

6. Take one cattail leaf and run it between your thumb and first finger to remove the excess water and air trapped inside the leaf. (Do this step each time that a leaf is taken out of the water.)

7. Thread the cattail leaf under the rubber band, *over the top* of the shoe box, and then *under* the rubber band on the opposite side of the box to keep it in place.

8. Thread another cattail leaf in the same way beside the first one, and repeat steps 6 and 7 until the top of the box is covered with leaves.

9. Turn the shoe box so that the two sides without cattail leaves can be seen.

10. Push a cattail leaf *under* the rubber band on one bare side of the box and then *under the first cattail leaf, over the next cattail leaf, under the next and over again* until reaching the end of the top of the box. Push the cattail leaf under the rubber band on the other side.

11. Push another cattail leaf under the rubber band just like in step 10, but this time begin *over the cattail leaf, under the next, and over again* until reaching the end. Push the cattail leaf under the rubber band on the other side to keep it in place.

12. Each new row of weaving begins opposite of the one before it. If the last row began *over,* then the next row will begin *under.*

13. Repeat the weaving process until the entire top of the box is covered with the cattail weaving.

14. Start with one cattail leaf to weave the sides of your basket. Weave over and under the cattails on the sides of your box. Snip off the cattail when reaching where weaving started, tuck it into the weaving and begin a new row.

15. Each row starts the opposite of the one before it. If the last row began *over,* then the next row starts *under.*

16. Keep weaving until the basket is as tall as desired. The top of the shoe box will be the bottom of the basket.

17. Snip off the cattails about two inches above the rubber band and remove the rubber band.

18. Turn the shoe box upside down and remove the basket.

19. Carefully bend the top pieces of cattail down and tuck them into the basket weaving.

**HINT:**
Use a sponge soaked with warm water to moisten the basket if it becomes too dry while working.

# CATTAIL WEAVING

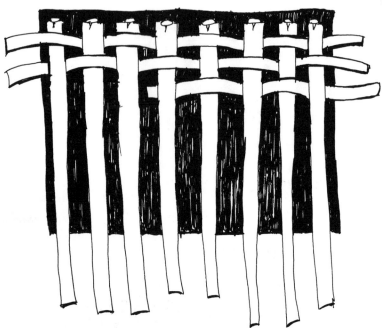

**PROCESS:**

1. Gather cattail leaves in swampy areas using heavy scissors. Cut them close to the base.

2. Spread cattails out on newspaper to dry in a warm, dry place until they become brownish-green in color (one to two weeks).

3. Soak dried cattails in water for at least 15 minutes before using.

4. Take a cattail from the water and run it between your thumb and first finger to remove the excess water and air trapped inside the leaf. Do this each time a leaf is taken from the water.

5. Lay cattail horizontally on cardboard and secure each end with a thumb tack. Cut it to the length desired.

6. Take several more cattails and lay them beside the first one and repeat step 5. The more cattails, the bigger the weaving.

7. Take another cattail leaf and thread it vertically **under** the bottom horizontal leaf then **over**, and **under again,** continuing until reaching the top.

8. Thread another cattail leaf vertically, but this time begin **over** the bottom horizontal leaf and **under** the next and **over** again until reaching the top.

9. Each new row of weaving begins opposite of the one before it.

10. Repeat the weaving process until there is a nice square or rectangular weaving.

11. Remove thumb tacks.

12. Carefully bend ends over and tuck them into the weaving.

13. Use the weaving as a placemat, rug, blanket, or wall hanging.

**MATERIALS:**

newspaper     thumb tacks or push pins
heavy scissors     piece of heavy cardboard
scissors     cattail leaves
tub or large container filled with water
sponge

**HINT:**
Use a sponge soaked with water to moisten the weaving if it becomes too dry.

# HOMEMADE BY HAND

chapter 5

# EARTH PAINTS

**MATERIALS:**

earth
pans
newspaper
rolling pin or hammer
plastic storage bags
sieve or sifter (the crank kind used to make applesauce is ideal)
bowl
tablespoon
butter knife or pallette knife
hard smooth surface (such as a piece of glass, the bottom of a metal pot, or a ceramic plate)
water
paper
paintbrushes
jars with lids

**PROCESS:**

1. Gather pans of soil and dirt from places around you. Look for places that are free from foliage, or are not too sandy. Ideal locations are barren fields, construction sites, quarry sites, or areas where roads have been cut through hillsides leaving soil exposed. Soil or earth comes in many colors from brick red to black.

2. Spread earth on newspaper and let dry thoroughly.

3. Place dried earth into a doubled plastic storage bag.

4. Crush with rolling pin or hammer.

5. Pour crushed earth into sieve or sifter with a bowl underneath the sieve. Strain particles of earth through the sieve or sifter, saving only the smallest pieces in the bowl.

6. Use the tablespoon to gather some of the earth particles from the bowl and place on a hard surface.

7. Add water (a few drops at a time) and mix with pallette knife into smooth paste like paint.

8. Dip paintbrush into earth paint to create a design or picture on paper.

9. Add water to thin paint as needed.

10. Store dry earth paints labeled in jars with lids.

**VARIATIONS:**

1. Try painting on woods, stone, or the smooth inside of a piece of bark.

2. Paint on newspaper, cardboard, grocery sacks, or paper scraps.

# EARTH CRAYONS

**MATERIALS:**
2 ounces of beeswax
2 ounces of paraffin
6 teaspoons or turpentine
3 to 5 ounces of natural pigment (see Earth Paints, page 182)
pan to melt wax
spoon to stir mixture
aluminum foil
cupcake cups
cupcake pan
stove

**PROCESS:**
1. Line the cupcake pan with aluminum foil and place paper cupcake cups into pan. (Adult supervision required for steps 1, 2, 3, and 4.)
2. Melt wax and paraffin in pan over low heat. (CAUTION)
3. Remove from heat.
4. Slowly add turpentine and dry earth pigment to warm wax mixture, and stir all ingredients until mixed.
5. Pour warm mixture into cupcake cups and let cool.
6. Remove crayons when cool.
7. Use as crayons.

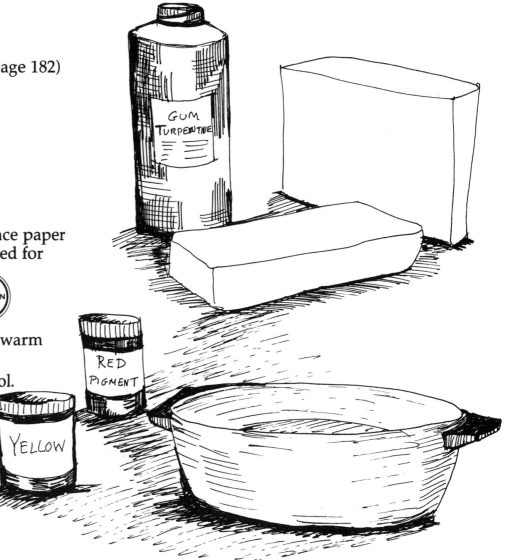

# ROLL-ON PAINTERS

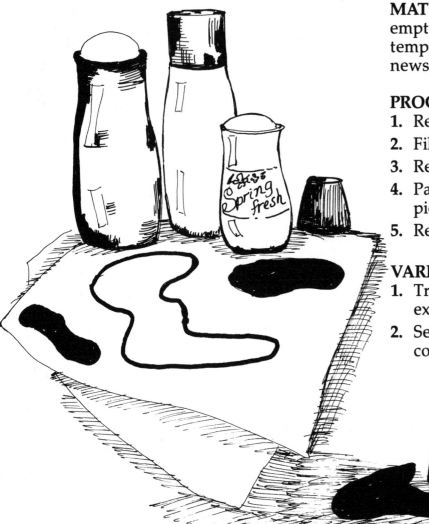

**MATERIALS:**
empty glass roll-on deodorant bottles, one for each color
tempera paint
newspaper or other paper

**PROCESS:**
1. Remove rollers from bottles, and clean roller and bottle.
2. Fill bottles with tempera paint.
3. Replace rollers.
4. Paint with roll-on painters making designs, drawing pictures, or enjoying the movement.
5. Refill as necessary.

**VARIATIONS:**
1. Try painting on different textures such as bumpy paper, extra smooth and shiny paper, or on cardboard.
2. Search for extra large and extra small rollers for your collection of bottles.

# NATURE PAINTBRUSH

**MATERIALS:**

pine branches
evergreen branches
Queen Anne's lace
feathers
twigs

ferns
hay
wheat
paint in shallow container
paper

**PROCESS:**

1. Dab evergreen branches into paint and then on paper.

2. Experiment with other items from nature for a variety of effects:
   Queen Anne's lace resembles a fireworks display!
   Twig end may be crushed to make a brush.
   Feathers may first be clipped in clothespins, or try using a feather duster.

3. If you prefer, collect broken or semi-dried plants rather than cutting living pieces for art.

**VARIATIONS:**

1. Use same materials for making crayon rubbings instead of painting with them.

2. When paintings are dry, add fingerprints, collage items, watercolor paint, glitter, or other craft items of your choice.

3. Tape, glue, or staple nature item to painting when done to be part of the art.

**WHAT ELSE TO SAVE FOR PAINTING:**

| | | | | |
|---|---|---|---|---|
| crumpled paper | yarn | vegetables | toy cars' wheels | kitchen utensils |
| clay | pieces of cardboard | squeeze bottles | corn cobs | cookie cutters |
| cotton balls | sticks | turkey baster | berry baskets | and more... |
| Q-tips | wood blocks | marbles | hardware tools | more...<br>and more! |

# 5 & up ⊘ ⊘ ⊛ HOMEMADE CHALK and BOARD

**MATERIALS:**
powdered tempera paint
½ cup water
3 tablespoons plaster of Paris
small paper cup
chalkboard paint
cardboard or masonite
cloth tape
sock

**PROCESS:**
**The Chalk:**
1. Mix paint, water, and plaster.
2. Pour into a small paper cup.
3. Dry for one hour or until hard.
4. Peel off the cup.
5. Draw, but experiment with surfaces to test for erasability.

**The Chalk Board:**
1. Brush or spray special chalkboard paint (from hobby or hardware stores) on a piece of cardboard or masonite.
2. Dry.
3. Trim edges of cardboard with cloth tape.
4. Use old sock over hand as an eraser.

# EGG SHELL CRAYONS

**MATERIALS:**
crayon stubs, paper removed
empty egg shells (half shells or large hole in top of egg)
can, set in pan partially filled with hot water

**PROCESS:**
1. Drop crayon stubs into can. Put can in pan of hot water.
2. Melt until squishy with little chunks floating.
3. Pour squishy, chunky wax into egg shells in egg carton. Fill to top.
4. Let cool and harden.
   (Place in freezer for quick hardening.)
5. Peel away egg shell.
6. Color with remaining egg-shaped crayon.
7. Store in egg carton.

**VARIATIONS:**
1. Melt crayon stubs in muffin tins in oven on low. Mix colors for a rainbow effect. (We call these "Scribble Cookies".)
2. Make larger "scribble pies" in small aluminum pie tins from frozen pot-pies.
3. Use old paint brush dipped in liquid crayons for a technique called "encaustic", whose result resembles oil painting.

CAUTION

# NATURAL FINGER PAINT

## MATERIALS:
½ cup finely chopped soap chips
1 cup cornstarch
6 cups water
large sauce pan
colored chalks, or chalk pastels (crushed)
storage containers with lids (margarine containers, glass jars)

## PROCESS:
1. In a large sauce pan combine the soap chips, cornstarch, and water.
2. Bring mixture to a boil over medium heat, stirring constantly. (Adult supervision suggested.) **CAUTION**
3. Remove when mixture has thickened.
4. Pour into individual containers.
5. Place one color of crushed chalk in each container and mix while it is still warm.
6. Let cool.
7. Store in covered containers.
8. Use as any finger paint by placing a dollop of the mixture on paper and smearing it around with hands and fingers.

## VARIATIONS:
**Add other textures, scents, or ingredients to any recipe and experiment with results. Try:**
    salt, coffee grounds, sand
    vanilla, cinnamon, perfume, liquid hand soap
    talcum powder
    glitter

# EASY FINGER PAINT

## RECIPE 1:
### MATERIALS:
3 parts water
1 part cornstarch
powdered (or liquid) tempera paint
pan

### PROCESS:
1. Boil water and remove from heat. CAUTION
2. Dissolve cornstarch in a little cold water and add to the hot water, stirring constantly. Boil until clear and thick (a minute or so).
3. Add powdered tempera paint. Experiment with food coloring if paint is not available.
4. Use, while still warm, on damp paper.

## RECIPE 2:
### MATERIALS:
½ cup liquid starch
powdered or liquid tempera paint
heavy paper

### PROCESS:
1. Pour a puddle of liquid starch on the paper.
2. Sprinkle a teaspoon or so of paint in center of puddle.
3. Mix and spread color with fingers and hands.
4. Paper can be dampened with water first for a slippery surface.

# HOMEMADE RICE PASTE

## MATERIALS:

rice
heavy aluminum foil or plastic wrap
hammer or rolling pin
storage container with a lid
   (margarine container or jar)
sauce pan with lid

stove
permanent marker
½ cup water
1 cup water
strainer or colander

## PROCESS:

1. Place about ½ cup of water into a container with a lid.
2. Pour in an equal amount of rice.
3. Cover and let the mixture stand for a week. Then drain off water.
4. Pour rice onto aluminum foil or heavy plastic wrap.
5. Crush rice with a hammer or rolling pin.
6. Pour rice, crushed, into a sauce pan with 1 cup of water which has been spread on a work surface.
7. Bring to a rolling boil, stirring constantly.
8. Reduce heat and simmer until mixture thickens.
9. Strain mixture with colander or strainer over storage container.
10. Allow the liquid to cool. This is the rice paste.
11. Cover with a lid and label the rice paste.

## VARIATIONS:

1. Use for pasting any paper.
2. Try adding color to rice paste and use for gluing collages of sand, grains, or paper.

# HOMEMADE FLOUR PASTE

**MATERIALS:**
1 part flour
1 part water
bowl
spoon

**PROCESS:**
1. Spoon a small amount of flour into a bowl.
2. Add an equal amount of water.
3. Mix together flour and water until mixture is smooth.
4. Add more water if the mixture is too stiff, or more flour if the mixture is too runny.
5. Use as paste for any paper.

**VARIATIONS:**
1. Make papier-mâché by dunking shredded paper into this paste and molding it over wood, balloons, or paper tubes.
2. Sculpt with paper dunked in paste by squeezing and building a design or shape. Then dry.

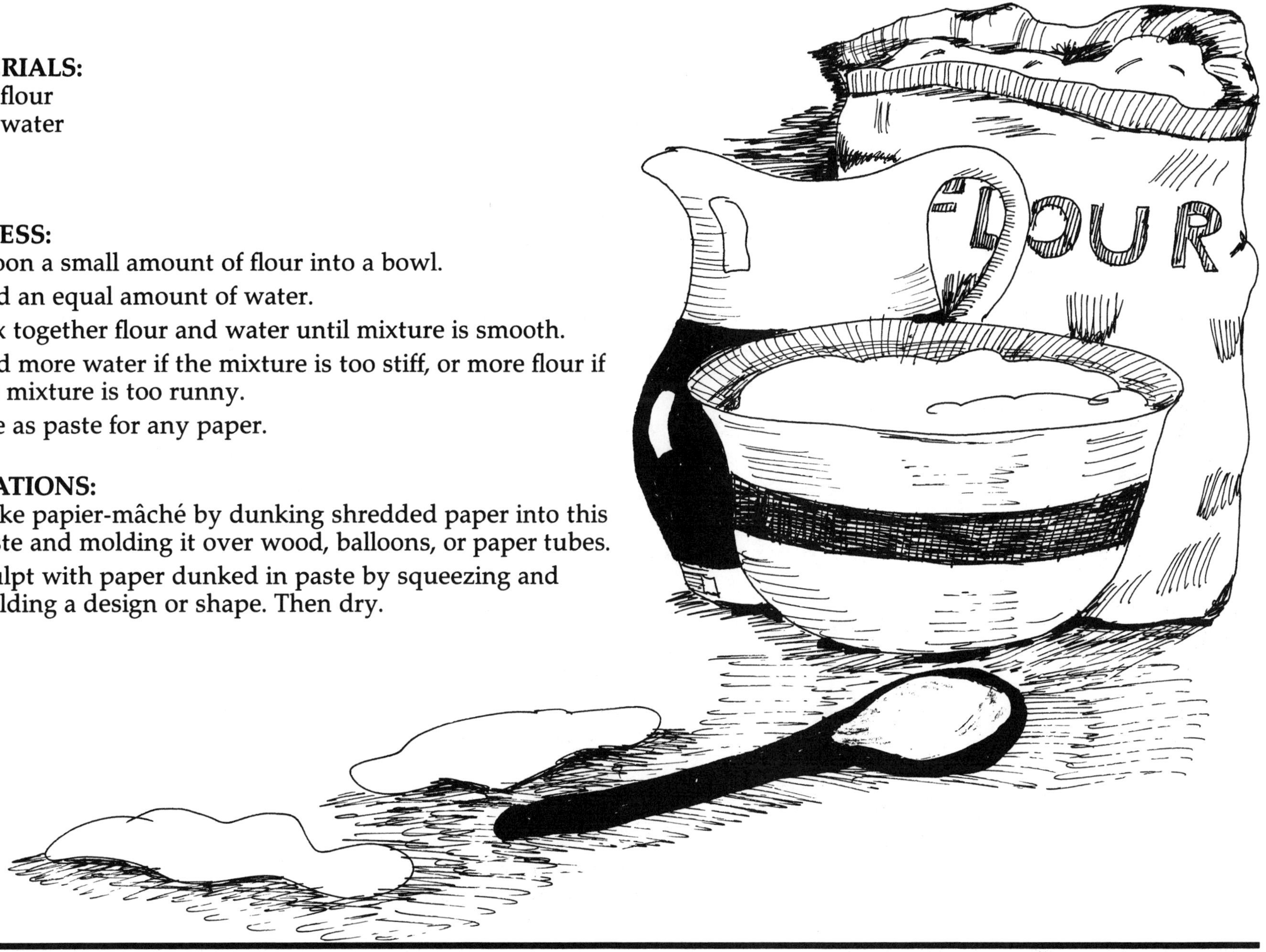

# HOMEMADE PAPER

**MATERIALS:**

newspapers
bucket
water
wire whisk
3 tablespoons of cornstarch

1 cup water
measuring spoons
piece of screen about 6″ across
rolling pin
sheet of plastic wrap to cover screen

**PROCESS:**

1. Tear newspapers into small pieces, filling bucket half full.
2. Add water, wetting paper pieces thoroughly. Let stand 2 hours.
3. Beat mixture into a creamy pulp with wire whisk.
4. Dissolve cornstarch in water.
5. Add cornstarch to pulp, and mix again.
6. Submerge piece of screen in pulp and pull it out.
7. Repeat #6 until the screen has about a 1/8″ thick layer of pulp.
8. Spread out some sheets of newspaper.
9. Lay pulp-covered screen on newspaper.
10. Cover screen with plastic wrap.
11. Press out excess water with rolling pin.
12. Set screen up so air can dry the pulp.
13. When dry, gently peel recycled paper from screen.
14. Use as a decorative piece of paper.

**VARIATIONS:**

1. Experiment with a large window screen and making a large piece of paper.
2. Mix a batch of paper in the blender or food processor, but reduce recipe to fit the appliance.

# HANDMADE LINT PAPER

**MATERIALS:**
lint from clothes dryer
  (large amounts can be obtained from laundromats)
cake pan
rags
cookie sheet
any of the following torn into small pieces: flowers, grasses,
  seeds, weeds, leaves, paper towels, colored paper, newspaper
water
wire mesh or old screen
heavy scissors
construction or poster paper
white glue

**PROCESS:**
1. Cut wire mesh or old screen into a circle that fits easily inside the cake pan. Remove.
2. Place lint and gathered materials into cake pan and fill with warm water.
3. Let stand for 5 minutes.
4. Submerge wire mesh or old screen into "lint soup".
5. Lift wire mesh out of mixture so that a layer of lint remains on top. Patch any holes in remaining lint mixture. Use fingers.
6. Blot lint paper carefully with rags.
7. Place on cookie sheet or pizza pan.
8. Let dry.
9. Remove from screen and glue lint paper to construction paper to see its beauty.

**VARIATIONS:**
1. To the lint mixture, add very tiny bits of colored thread, dried grass, or fabric pieces.
2. Glue dried paper to used paper and mat or frame.

# RECYCLED WRAP

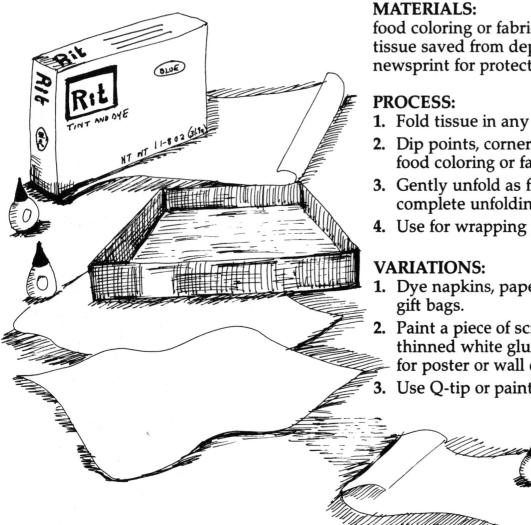

**MATERIALS:**
food coloring or fabric dye (Rit works well)
tissue saved from department store boxes
newsprint for protecting table

**PROCESS:**
1. Fold tissue in any fashion.
2. Dip points, corners, or edges into cups filled with diluted food coloring or fabric dye.
3. Gently unfold as far as possible. Let tissue dry and then complete unfolding.
4. Use for wrapping paper.

**VARIATIONS:**
1. Dye napkins, paper towels, or facial tissues and use to stuff gift bags.
2. Paint a piece of scrap poster board with liquid starch or thinned white glue. Press dyed paper to board. Dry. Use for poster or wall decoration.
3. Use Q-tip or paintbrush to paint paper with dye.

# WRAPPINGS AND BOWS

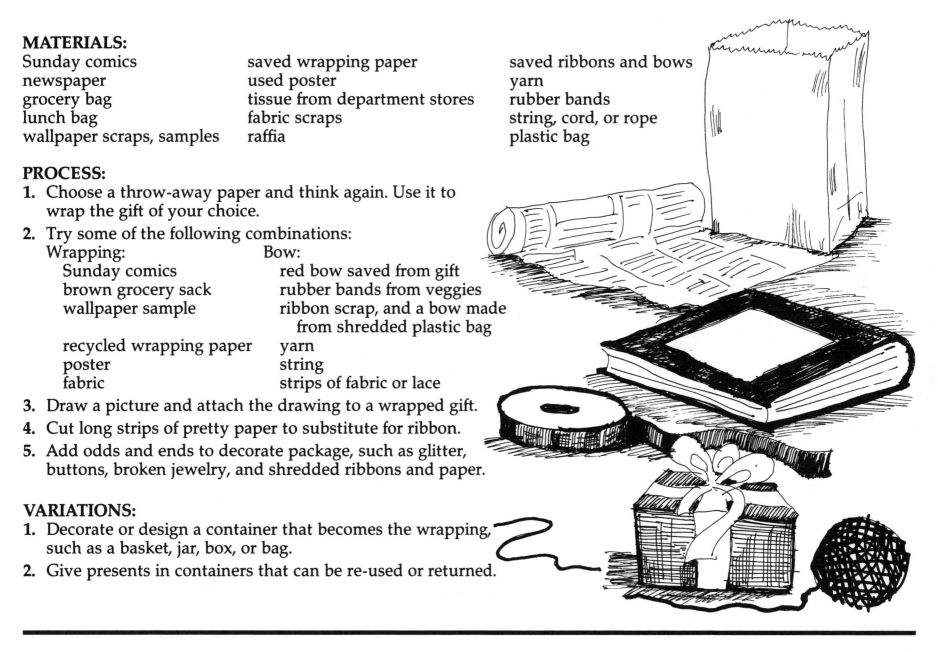

**MATERIALS:**

Sunday comics
newspaper
grocery bag
lunch bag
wallpaper scraps, samples

saved wrapping paper
used poster
tissue from department stores
fabric scraps
raffia

saved ribbons and bows
yarn
rubber bands
string, cord, or rope
plastic bag

**PROCESS:**

1. Choose a throw-away paper and think again. Use it to wrap the gift of your choice.

2. Try some of the following combinations:

   Wrapping:
   - Sunday comics
   - brown grocery sack
   - wallpaper sample

   - recycled wrapping paper
   - poster
   - fabric

   Bow:
   - red bow saved from gift
   - rubber bands from veggies
   - ribbon scrap, and a bow made from shredded plastic bag

   - yarn
   - string
   - strips of fabric or lace

3. Draw a picture and attach the drawing to a wrapped gift.

4. Cut long strips of pretty paper to substitute for ribbon.

5. Add odds and ends to decorate package, such as glitter, buttons, broken jewelry, and shredded ribbons and paper.

**VARIATIONS:**

1. Decorate or design a container that becomes the wrapping, such as a basket, jar, box, or bag.

2. Give presents in containers that can be re-used or returned.

# NATURAL BERRY DYE

**MATERIALS:**
berries (preferably fresh)
cooking pot (stainless steel, glass, or enamel) with lid
stove
storage containers with lids (such as milk cartons, glass jars, or margarine containers)
water
spoon
colander or strainer
large mixing bowl

**PROCESS:**
1. Gather fresh berries.
2. Place berries into cooking pot.
3. Add water.
   (Hints: More berries will make a stronger dye. Do not use less than one cup of berries to a pint of water, or two cups per quart of water.)
4. Cover mixture with lid.
5. Bring to a boil.
6. Reduce heat and simmer between 45 minutes to an hour, stirring occasionally. (CAUTION)
7. Remove from heat and cool.
8. Strain off berries with strainer or colander over a bowl.
9. Reserve colored liquid in large mixing bowl.
10. Pour colored dye into storage containers.

**VARIATIONS:**
Experiment making dye colors using cranberries, grapes, onion skins, beets, spinach leaves, tea bags, or instant coffee. See page 197, "Natural Dyes: Sources" for color suggestions.

# NATURAL DYES: SOURCES

Almost any plant materials will yield some type of dye when boiled. Plants listed below are rich sources of color. The colors listed are an approximation of dye results depending on how much plant is used.

Experiment with plants in your own backyard or neighborhood such as dandelions. You can always buy some cranberries or onions at the market. Take a look in your garden, too. Spinach and beets make wonderful dyes.

For a source of plants with easy to use pictures, see the Reader's Digest *Magic and Medicine of Plants*, 1986. There are other various field guides available to take on walks to help identify plants you find.

| Plant — | Use the — | Color — |
|---|---|---|
| All berries: blackberries, raspberries, cranberries, blueberries | berries | variety |
| Agrimony | leaves and stalks | peach |
| Alkanet | roots | brown |
| Beets | leaves and roots | pinkish-green |
| Bloodroot | roots | dusty rose |
| Broom | flowers | peach |
| Celandine | flowers | yellow |
| Comfrey | leaves | yellow |
| Dandelion | flowers | yellow |
| Dandelion | roots | yellow |
| Elderberry | berries | lavendar |
| Fenugreek | seeds | yellow-brown |
| Goldenrod | flowers | yellow-gold |
| Heather | tips | green |
| Hyssop | leaves | dark green |
| Lily of the Valley | leaves and stalks | spring green |
| Mullein | leaves and stalks | gold |
| Onion (yellow) | skins | light brown |
| Onion (red) | skins | red-brown |
| Parsley | leaves | light green |
| Privet | leaves and twigs | light green |
| Queen Anne's Lace | flowers and stalks | yellow |
| Smartweed | all but roots | yellow-green |
| Spinach | leaves | green |
| Stinging nettle | all but roots | light brown |
| Tansy | flowers | yellow |
| Yarrow | flowers | light green |

# KOOL-AID DYES

**MATERIALS:**
packages of unsweetened Kool-Aid or powdered drink mix
stainless steel, glass or enamel cooking pot with lid
½ cup white vinegar
½ gallon water
stove
storage containers with lids for dyes (glass jars, plastic
   margarine containers)
remnant of raw wool, square of white wool, piece of cotton, or
   white cotton handkerchief

**PROCESS:**
1. Pour two packages of unsweetened Kool-Aid or powdered
   drink mix into cooking pot.
2. Add vinegar and water.
3. Cover and heat until pot steams.
4. Simmer for 20 to 30 minutes.
5. Let cool.
6. Pour dyes into storage containers.

**TO USE:**
1. Wet wool or cotton.
2. Dip into dye.

**VARIATIONS:**
1. Paint dye on fabric with brush or Q-tip.
2. Draw on fabric with crayon, then dip in dye for a batik effect.
3. See Tie-Dye, page 199 and Recycled Wrap, page 194.
4. Experiment with dyeing papers, such as napkins or tissue.

# TIE-DYE

**MATERIALS:**
Natural Berry or Kool-Aid Dyes (see pages 196 and 198)
pieces of cotton fabric or white cotton handkerchief
rubber bands or string
spoons or squeeze bottles (plastic ketchup or syrup bottles)
scissors
bowls

**PROCESS:**
1. Fold cotton fabric or handkerchief into a small square, diamond, spiral, or rectangle.
2. Secure tightly with rubber bands or string.
3. Apply dyes to cloth with spoons, or squeeze dye in areas with squeeze bottles. (Dyes can also be applied by dipping the cloth into a bowl filled with dye.)
4. Next, cut off strings or remove rubber bands.
5. Unfold cloth carefully.
6. Let dry.

**VARIATIONS:**
1. Staple or tape tie-dye fabric to a heavy white mat board for display.
2. Try dyeing the following papers by dipping into dye:
   piece of heavy paper folded tightly
   folded coffee filter
   folded white tissue
   folded napkins or paper towels

# NATURAL EGG DYES

## MATERIALS:

eggs
mild soap and water
towel
plastic sandwich bags
bag twists, rubber bands, or string
cooking pot
stove
natural materials to make egg dyes
   (berries, spinach leaves, tea bags)

## PROCESS:

1. Wash egg gently with mild soap and water, and towel dry.
2. Fill a plastic sandwich bag with any of the dye materials and a small amount water.
3. Place egg in sandwich bag. (Close the bag tightly with a bag twist, rubber band, or string.)
4. Place sandwich bag into cooking pot filled with water.
5. Boil 10 minute, then cool.
6. Remove the bag from the cool water. **CAUTION**
7. Untie the bag and remove egg. Different colors will be left on the egg from the natural materials.

## VARIATIONS:

1. Draw with white crayon on egg before dyeing.
2. Hard-cook egg before dyeing to help prevent breakage.
3. Experiment with a variety of natural materials to achieve a variety of colors.

# ONION SKIN EGG DYE

**MATERIALS:**
eggs
brown or purple onion skin
small leaves
squares of old cloth or foot of nylon stocking
rubber bands
pot filled with water

**PROCESS:**
1. Place cloth on table.
2. Place 6 layers of onion skin on top of cloth.
3. Place leaves on top of onion skins.
4. Place egg on top of leaves and onion skins.
5. Place more onion skins on top of egg.
6. Wrap cloth around egg packet tightly, placing rubber bands around and around egg.
7. Place wrapped egg in pot of boiling water for 30 minutes.
8. Remove. Cool.
9. Remove cloth and materials.
10. Dry.
11. Rub with cooking oil for shiny appearance.

**CAUTION**

**VARIATIONS:**
1. Use eggs for a centerpiece in a basket.
2. Add other colors to egg with felt pens.

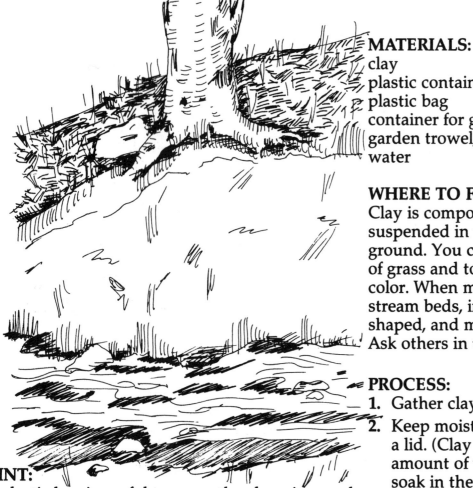

**HINT:**
A plastic bag is useful to cover the clay piece and keep it from drying out if the modeling process is not complete.

**NOTE:**
See page 204, Basic Natural Kiln, for firing suggestions.

**MATERIALS:**
clay
plastic container with a tight-fitting lid
plastic bag
container for gathering clay
garden trowel, shovel, or other digging tools
water

**WHERE TO FIND CLAY:**
Clay is composed of very fine particles of earth which are suspended in water. It occurs in natural deposits under the ground. You can usually find a deposit of clay beneath layers of grass and topsoil. It can be yellow, red, brown, or grayish in color. When moist, it is pliable. Clay can also be found along stream beds, in fields, or on hillsides. Clay can be gathered, shaped, and made permanent through a process called firing. Ask others in the art world where they find their clay.

**PROCESS:**
1. Gather clay.
2. Keep moist clay from drying out in a plastic container with a lid. (Clay that is too dry can be used again if a small amount of water is added to the dry clay and allowed to soak in the moisture for several hours or overnight.)
3. Knead the moist clay to make it more pliable and remove air bubbles. (This is called wedging the clay.)
4. Shape the clay into desired shape.
5. Let the clay dry in its modeled form. (This is called greenware.)
6. Fire the clay for permanence, or moisten the clay for re-use by adding water in the plastic container to the dry clay.

# CLAY PINCH POT

**MATERIALS:**
moist clay
your hands
twig (optional)

**PROCESS:**
1. Form clay into a ball.
2. Push one thumb into the center of the clay, but not through it.
3. Cup one hand underneath the clay, and use the other to turn the clay and pinch it with your thumb and forefinger. The opening of the pot will get larger and larger until a pinch pot is formed.

**VARIATIONS:**
1. Try scratching a design into the sides of the pinch pot with a twig or fingers.
2. Try making a pot formed with coils or strings of clay (Blend coils together inside the pot.)
3. Try making free-form sculpture or clay designs.

# BASIC NATURAL KILN

A kiln is an oven or fire used to bake clay to make it permanent. This process is called firing. Kilns get very hot. *Never* try to make or use a kiln without an adult to supervise.

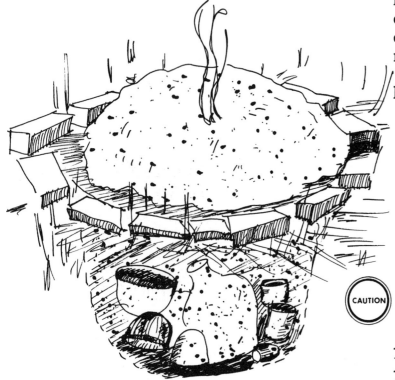

**MATERIALS:**
shovel
piece of ground to build a fire on
buckets of sand
fire brick or common brick
dry sawdust
dry twigs and grasses, dry leaves or dry hay
matches

**PROCESS:**
1. Dig a hole in the ground with a shovel deep enough to cover your greenware (dry clay ware).
2. Line the hole with sand.
3. Place greenware in the hole.
4. Layer greenware with sawdust and small, dry twigs.
5. Mound sawdust over greenware.
6. Mound hay or dry leaves and twigs over sawdust.
7. Line mound with a circle of fire brick or common brick.
8. Have an adult light with matches.
9. Allow fire to burn slowly. Watch it carefully, and keep buckets of sand close by in case of emergency.
10. Let fire cool.
11. Remove clay pieces.

**NOTE**
1. See Natural Clay, page 202, to form object for firing.
2. See Clay Pinch Pot, page 203, for clay technique.

# HOMEMADE FOSSILS

## MATERIALS:
soil
water
waxed paper
cookie sheet
mixing containers
spoon
small items:
    shells
    leaves
    wood
    pebbles

## PROCESS:
1. Fill a container half full with soil.
2. Mix water into soil until thick and hand-moldable.
   (Note: Potting soil is too dry to work well, so try to find
   some dirt with clay in it.)
3. Stir in little items such as shells and pebbles.
4. Mold a mudpie with small items completely concealed in mud.
5. Allow mudpies to dry for a full day and overnight.
6. When completely dry, break mudpie open with hands.
7. Look at the homemade fossil.

## VARIATIONS:
1. Put a lot of time into planning how the fossil will turn out.
2. Do rubbings of the fossil.
3. Make a plaster casting of a fossil.

# HOMEMADE PERFUME

**MATERIALS:**
hammer
waxed paper
lemons, limes, apples, herbs, mint leaves
blossoms of scented flowers
containers
water

**PROCESS:**
1. Crush foods with a hammer on pieces of waxed paper.
2. Place crushed foods into container.
3. Add water to cover overnight.
4. Pour off clear juice into different containers.
5. Use within a few days.

**VARIATIONS:**
1. Decorate a baby food jar and give perfume as a gift to someone special.
2. Experiment with mixing foods, herbs, and flowers to make unique scents.

# HOMEMADE CANDLES

**MATERIALS:**
cardboard juice can or milk carton
used candles

**PROCESS:**
1. First attach a thin candle for a wick, anchoring it by warming the end of the candle, and sticking it in the bottom of your container. (Adult supervision required for steps 1, 2, and 3.)
2. Melt used candles in an old pan or coffee can, set in a pan of warm water on the stove at medium heat.
3. Pour the warm wax into the container.
4. Candle will harden in 6 to 8 hours.
5. Peel away container.
6. Thin candle for wick may need trimming, or let it burn down to correct height.

**VARIATIONS:**
1. For striped candles, let layers of different colors harden before pouring in the next layer.
2. For a sand candle, use an indentation in the sand to pour your used, melted candles. The indentation will be your container.
3. Put ice cubes in a milk carton before pouring wax in. The ice will melt and leave a lacy, hole-y design.

# SAND DRIED FLOWERS

**MATERIALS:**

| | |
|---|---|
| box | drinking straws |
| sand | pipecleaners |
| scissors | green paper |
| fresh flowers | white glue |

**PROCESS:**
1. Fill box half-full with sand.
2. Cut the stem of each flower to as long as your middle finger.
3. Push the flower stem into the sand.
4. Gently sprinkle sand over the flowers, covering them completely.
   (Hint: You may need to open petals a bit and sprinkle sand inside the blossom.)
5. Leave box in a dry place for two weeks.
6. When dry, gently tilt box and pour out the top sand.
7. Lift flowers out gently.
8. You can attach flowers to a drinking straw with a pipecleaner, or use as is.
9. If you like, cut green leaves from paper and glue to the stems.

**VARIATIONS:**
1. Use dried flowers for nature sculptures, centerpieces, or other projects calling for decorations from nature.
2. Make a bouquet or garland.

# SAND BAKED FLOWERS

CAUTION · 8 & up

**MATERIALS:**
1 or more rectangular kitchen pans
fine sand
fresh flowers
paper
soft brush
box

**PROCESS:**
1. Fill a pan 1 inch deep with sand.
2. Place flowers face down in sand.
3. Carefully push sand under the petals so they will not dry flat.
4. Pour another inch of sand over the flowers, carefully.
5. Bake in 200° oven for about two hours.
   (Note: Some flowers take longer or shorter time than others. To test, pour off a little sand from the corner of the pan. If flowers look dark or dull, they have baked too long. If flowers look damp or droopy, they need more baking. Flowers baked just the right amount of time will look like they did before you baked them.)
6. Pour off sand carefully.
7. Put flowers on paper for about an hour to regain some softness.
8. Brush all remaining sand from flower petals with a soft brush.
9. Store dried flowers face down in a cardboard box until needed.
10. Use for any project asking for dried flowers, such as placing in a decorated jar.

# GLYCERIN PRESERVING

**MATERIALS:**
branch with leaves (green or just changing color)
newsprint
hammer
1 part glycerin from craft or drugstore
2 parts water in large jar

**PROCESS:**
1. Lay the branch on layers of newsprint.
2. Crush the end of the stem with the hammer until soft.
3. Mix one part glycerin in two parts water in the jar.
4. Stick the branch in the glycerin mixture for about two weeks.
5. When the leaves have become thick and color has changed, they are ready.
6. Display the leaves in any project calling for leaves.

**VARIATIONS:**
1. Cover a coffee can or juice can and put branch in the can to enjoy.
2. Decorate the branch with other items such as paper flowers, pine cones, or weeds and reeds.

# PRESSED PLANTS

**MATERIALS:**
fresh wildflowers, leaves, or other plants
heavy books
newspaper
white glue
poster board or heavy paper

**PROCESS:**
1. Gather fresh leaves, wildflowers, and other plants from fields or wooded areas.
2. Spread newspaper over a hard, flat surface.
3. Arrange plants, leaves, and wildflowers on the newspaper.
4. Cover plants with another piece of newspaper.
5. Place heavy books or objects over the plants so plants can dry out for about two weeks.
6. Use pressed plants and white glue to make a picture or design.
7. Glue pressed plants to heavy paper, posterboard, or cardboard.

**VARIATIONS:**
**Use pressed plants for:**
   decorating note cards
   decorating a gift box
   pressing between waxed paper
   pressing between clear contact paper

# POTPOURRI

**MATERIALS:**
spices (cinnamon, ginger, cloves, or anise)
fresh flowers (find flowers with a scent)
nylon stocking, piece of cheese cloth, or netting
scissors
ribbon or string

**PROCESS:**
1. Pull apart flowers.
2. Crush spices if they are fresh.
3. Cut foot off stocking with scissors (or cut cheese cloth into a small circle).
4. Place flowers and spices into stocking or cheese cloth.
5. Tie securely with ribbon or string.
6. Use as a purse fragrance, place in a drawer, or give as a gift.

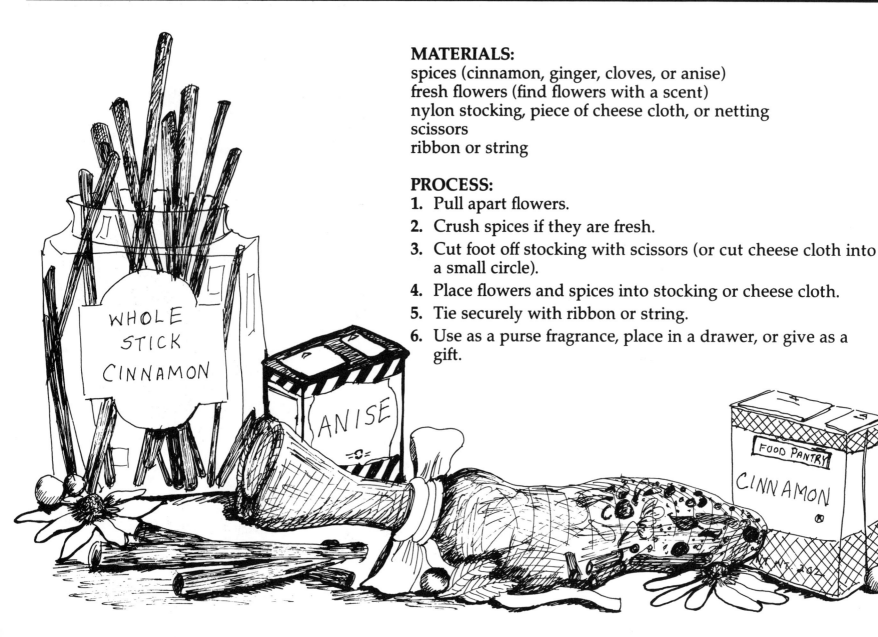

# HOMEMADE T-SHIRT YARN

**MATERIALS:**
old T-shirt (not double-knit)
scissors

**PROCESS:**
1. Trim away hem of shirt.
2. Cut away any pockets or decoration.
3. Cut all around the T-shirt in a spiral. (This makes a long, continuous strip of fabric.)
4. By stretching the strip, the edges will curl and strip will resemble yarn.
5. To store, wrap "yarn" in a ball or skein.

**USE FOR:**
   weaving projects
   wrapping presents
   hanging mobiles
   any projects needing yarn or string

**VARIATIONS:**
1. Stuff old shirt with fluff, sew openings, and use for a pillow.
2. Sew neck hole and arm holes. Add a shoulder strap and use shirt for carry bag. Decorate with fabric crayons, if desired.

# OLD SOCK PUPPETS

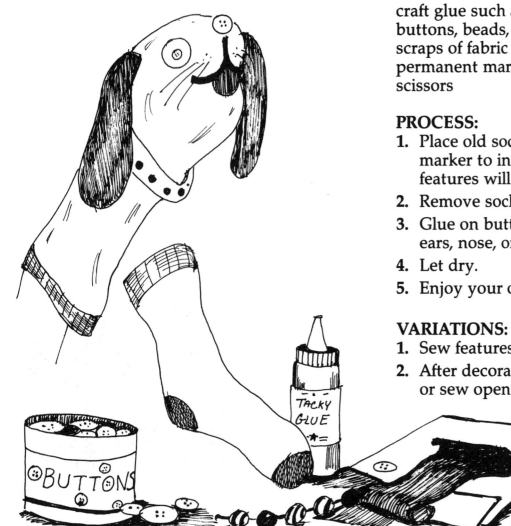

**MATERIALS:**
old socks
craft glue such as Tacky or Sobo glue
buttons, beads, or yarn
scraps of fabric
permanent markers
scissors

**PROCESS:**
1. Place old sock over hand and make dots with permanent marker to indicate where eyes, ears, and other body features will be.
2. Remove sock from hand.
3. Glue on buttons, fabric scraps, beads, or yarn to form eyes, ears, nose, or other body features.
4. Let dry.
5. Enjoy your original sock puppet.

**VARIATIONS:**
1. Sew features to sock instead of gluing.
2. After decorating sock, stuff with paper or fabric scraps. Tie or sew opening closed to make puppet into a doll or toy.

# RESOURCE GUIDE

chapter 6

# WHERE TO FIND FREE MATERIALS

**Advice for the "gatherer":**

When a listing says "save", collect this material from a friend, a classroom, an office, or garage sale. Also, garage sales and thrift stores are often listed as excellent sources for materials or supplies, and although not free, they often will give you items for almost free when you mention the use is for children's art. Don't be afraid to ask!

Most businesses, fast food restaurants, banks, and grocery stores will donate a small amount of whatever you need for a project.

These materials can be recycled from their trash rather than new: paper, styrofoam trays, straws and stir-sticks, plastic and paper bags, rubber bands, scrap wood, shredded paper, paint, cans, wire, sand, wall-paper and sample books, and more! Simply ask and explain its use – for example, for a child to make a sculpture. If you need enough for a group, offer to pay. Usually no payment is expected other than to credit their establishment when you can. Always ask those near you to save in advance for special projects. And save your own used materials too.

bags, grocery –
  save
  grocery store
  garage sale

beeswax –
  orthodontist office

bows –
  save
  garage sale

boxes –
  save
  moving company
  appliance store
  construction site
  bookstore
  liquor store
  school
  grocery store

buttons –
  save
  garage sale
  laundromat

cans –
  save
  school cafeteria
  restaurant
  garage sale

coat hangers –
  save
  cleaners
  laundromat
  garage sale

construction materials –
  save
  building sites
  lumber yard
  hardware store

containers, plastic tub –
  save
  garage sales
  restaurant
  school cafeteria

cups –
  save
  restaurant
  kitchen supplier
  catering service
  school

fabric –
  save
  fabric store
  quilter's scraps
  garage sale
  upholstery store
  factory that uses fabric

jewelry, beads –
  save
  garage sales
  thrift stores

illustration board (mat board) –
  frame shop scraps (label a box with your name for framer to save scraps for you)
  art gallery
  graphic artist studio

milk cartons, plastic or paper –
  save
  school cafeteria
  garage sale

newspaper, or newsprint –
  save
  newspaper print shop
  moving company

paints, all kinds –
  save
  garage sale
  auto repair shop
  house painter
  artist

paper, all kinds –
  save
  print shop's recycle bins
  copy shop
  office's recycle bins
  school's recycle bins
  moving company
  computer print-outs, office
  financial/investment office
  bank (great for shredded paper)

posters, poster paper –
  save
  video rental store
  grocery store
  printer's recycle bins (label a box with your name for printer to save paper for you)

junk mail –
  garage sale
  mall stores

ribbons –
  save
  floral shop
  off old clothing
  garage sale
  fabric store

styrofoam packing (peanuts) –
  save
  bookstore
  appliance store
  electronics store
  computer store

styrofoam trays –
  save
  garage sale
  grocery store

wire –
  save
  telephone installer
  floral shop
  feed supply store

wood scraps –
  save
  construction site
  high school shop class
  frame shop
  garage sale
  lumberyard
  crates (grocery store)

# ENVIRONMENTAL ORGANIZATIONS AND RESOURCES

*Alliance to Save Energy* (1725 K St NW, #914, Washington, DC 20006; 202-857-0666) has a free poster and guide to help you conserve energy in your home.

*Burpee* (02224497 Burpee Building, Warminster, PA 18974) carries fruit trees and shrubs and 400 different vegetables and 800 flowers. Free catalog and sometimes sample seeds.

*Center for Marine Conservation* (1725 DeSales St NW, #500, Washington, DC 20036; 202-429-5609) has a K-6 ocean activity book ($8.95) and an Adopt-a-Beach program.

*The Children's Rainforest* (PO Box 936, Lewiston, ME 04240, no phone) has free information to help you raise money to protect an acre of rainforest. Send a S.A.S.E.

*Citizens Clearinghouse for Hazardous Wastes* (PO Box 926, Arlington, VA 22216; 703-276-7070) has a membership focusing on hazardous wastes in your own neighborhoods with a publication for information.

*Co-Op America* (2100 M St NW, #310, Washington, DC 20063; 202-872-5307) provides catalogs of environmentally sound products to members. Other services. Non-profit.

*Coastal Conservation Association* (Amy Richard, PO Box 1630, Fulton, TX 78358; 512-729-7426) offers a free kids' magazine with a $10 membership fee. Deals with underwater ecosystems and how to become involved in your part of the country.

*Costeau Society* (930 W 21st ST, Norfolk, VA 23517; 804-627-1144) has a free subscription to "The Dolphin Log", a magazine dealing with human impact upon the sea. Family membership $28, or $10 a year for the magazine only.

*Hug the Earth* (PO Box 621, Wayne, PA 19087; 215-688-0566) sponsors monthly workshops and activities while helping kids understand the environment. Family membership with newsletter, $15 a year; classroom memberships, $1 per student.

*National Audubon Society* (950 Third Ave, New York, NY 10022; 212-832-3200) offers a $20/year membership to support efforts in conservation of all wildlife and land resources. Includes television specials, education centers, summer ecology camps, and field seminars.

*National Wildlife Federation* (1400 16th St NW, Washington, DC 20036; 202-797-6800) has a nature education catalog that has videos, games, books, kits, and information. Also has a free "Backyard Habitat" kit which teaches how to build a nest box for birds and how to encourage animals to choose your yard as a habitat.

*Seventh Generation* (Products for a Healthy Planet, 10 Farrell St, S Burlington, VT 05403; 800-456-1177) offers a full line of environmentally sound products through its mail order catalog. One percent of gross sales are donated to environmental groups. Membership entitles you to a 5% discount on their items, gives you a newsletter, tee shirt, and four catalogs.

*Sierra Club* (730 Polk St, San Francisco, CA 94109; 415-776-2211) has a 25¢ kids' packet which lists environmental organizations with kids' programs.

*Trees for Life* (1103 Jefferson, Wichita, KS 67203; 316-263-7294) has a tree-planting packet for $2. Includes seeds, instructions, information, container, and poster. For $1 each, they have buttons which help support Trees for Life projects in other countries.

*US Department of Agriculture* (US Forest Service, PO Box 96090, Washington, DC 20250; 202-447-4543) has a poster about leaves changing color and a booklet about how a tree grows.

*US Department of Energy* (Conservation and Renewable Energy Inquiry Referral Service, PO Box 8900, Silver Spring, MD 20907; 800-523-2929) offers a free brochure about energy conservation (#FS218) with helpful tips and pictures to color.

*US Environmental Protection Agency* (Office of Communications and Public Affairs, 401 M St SW, PM211B, Washington, DC 20460; 202-382-2080) can send free booklets on a variety of topics including acid rain, pollution, and recycling. Also has a coloring book.

*Whale Center* (3933 Piedmont Ave, Ste #2, Oakland CA 94611; 415-654-6621) has an "adopt a gray whale calf" program for kids for $25. You get a photo of a whale calf, adoption certificate, quarterly updates, and activity pages.

# BIBLIOGRAPHY

Allison, Linda. *TRASH ARTISTS WORKSHOP*. Belmont, CA: David S. Lake Publishers, 1981.
ISBN 0-8224-9780-8

Bartlett, Nancy Lewis. *CHILDREN'S ART AND CRAFTS*. The Australian Women's Weekly Home Library. ISBN 0 949128 01 5

Blakey, Nancy. *THE MUDPIES ACTIVITY BOOK*. Seattle, WA: Northwest Parent Publishing, Inc., 1989. ISBN 0-9614626-1-2

Bliss, Anne. *A HANDBOOK OF DYES FROM NATURAL MATERIALS*. New York: Charles Scribner's Sons, 1981. ISBN 0-684-16502-3

Brown, Sam Ed. *BUBBLES RAINBOWS & WORMS*. Mt.Rainier, MD: Gryphon House, 1981.
ISBN 0-87659-100-4

Bruno, Louis. *ELEMENTARY ART GUIDE*. Olympia, WA: Superintendent of Public Instruction, State of Washington, 1961.

Caney, Steven. *TOY BOOK*. New York: Workman Publishing Company, 1972.
ISBN 0-911104-17-8

Carson, Mary Stetten. *THE SCIENTIFIC KID*. New York: Harper and Row, Publishers, 1989.
ISBN 0-06-096316-6

Cobb, Vicki. *ARTS AND CRAFTS YOU CAN EAT*. Philadelphia: JB Lippincott Company, 1974.
ISBN 0-397-31492-2

Cooke, Viva and Sampley, Julia. *PALMETTO BRAIDING AND WEAVING*. Peoria, IL: Manual Arts Press, 1947.

Dobelis, Inge N. *MAGIC AND MEDICINE OF PLANTS*. Pleasantville, NY: Reader's Digest General Books, 1986. ISBN 0-89577-221-3

Earth*Works Group, The. *50 SIMPLE THINGS YOU CAN DO TO SAVE THE EARTH*. Berkeley, CA: Earth Works Press, 1989. ISBN 0-929634-06-03

Elkington, John. *GOING GREEN*. New York: A Puffin Book, 1990. ISBN 0-14-034597-3

Faggella, Kathy. *CRAYONS CRAFTS AND CONCEPTS*. Bridgeport, CT: First Teacher Press, 1985. ISBN 0-9615005-0-6

Fiarotta, Phyllis. *SNIPS & SNAILS & WALNUT WHALES*. New York: Workman Publishing Company, 1975. ISBN 0-911104-49-6

Gibson, Ray. *ODDS & ENDS*. London: Usborne Publishing Ltd., 1990. ISBN 0-7460-0633-0

Gilbreath, Alice. *SPOUTS, LIDS, AND CANS*. New York: William Morrow and Company, Inc., 1973. ISBN 0-688-20064-8

Haas, Carolyn Buhai. *RECIPES FOR FUN*. Northfield, IL: cbh publishing, inc., 1980.
ISBN 0-9604538-3-0

Haas, Carolyn Buhai. *LOOK AT ME*. Chicago: Chicago Review Press Incorporated, 1987.
ISBN 1-55652-021-2

Harris, Mark. *EMBRACING THE EARTH*. Chicago, IL: The Noble Press, 1990.
ISBN 0-9622683-2-1

Hill, Janis and Patrick, Laure. *FROM KIDS WITH LOVE*. Belmont, CA: David S. Lake Publishers, 1987. ISBN 0-8224-3166-1

*INSTRUCTOR'S ARTFULLY EASY*. New York: Instructor Books, 1983.

Kohl, MaryAnn F. *SCRIBBLE COOKIES AND OTHER INDEPENDENT CREATIVE ART EXPERIENCES FOR CHILDREN*. Bellingham, WA: Bright Ring Publishing, 1985.
ISBN 0-935607-10-2

Kohl, MaryAnn F. *MUDWORKS: CREATIVE CLAY, DOUGH, AND MODELING EXPERIENCES*. Bellingham, WA: Bright Ring Publishing, 1989. ISBN 0-935607-02-1

Lidstone, John. *BUILDING WITH CARDBOARD*. New York: Van Nostrand Reinhold Company, 1968.

Lohf, Sabine. *NATURE CRAFTS*. Chicago: Children's Press, Inc., 1990. ISBN 0-516-49257-8

Mack, Norman. *BACK TO BASICS*. Pleasantville, NY: The Reader's Digest Association, Inc., 1981. ISBN 0-89577-086-5

Miller, Karen. *THE OUTSIDE PLAY AND LEARNING BOOK*. Mt.Rainier, MD: Gryphon House, 1989. ISBN 0-87659-117-9

Milord, Susan. *THE KIDS' NATURE BOOK*. Charlotte, VT: Williamson Publishing.
ISBN 0-913589-42-X

Nelson, Glenn C. *A POTTER'S HANDBOOK*. New York: Holt, Rinehart, and Winston, 1971.
ISBN 0-03-022725-9

Robertson, Seonaid. *DYES FROM PLANTS*. New York: Van Nostrand Reinhold Company, 1973. ISBN 0-442-26974-9

Rockwell, Robert E. *HUG A TREE*. Mt.Rainier, MD: Gryphon House, 1986. ISBN 0-87659-105-5

Schiller, Pam and Rossano, Joan. *THE INSTANT CURRICULUM*. Mt. Rainier, MD: Gryphon House, 1990. ISBN 0-87659-124-1

Schwartz, Linda. *EARTH BOOK FOR KIDS*. Santa Barbara, CA: The Learning Works, Inc., 1990.
ISBN 0-88160-195-0

Seyd, Mary. *INTRODUCING BEADS*. London: B.T. Batsford Limited, 1973. ISBN 0-8230-6128

Sherwood, Elizabeth, Williams, Robert A., Rockwell, Robert. *MORE MUDPIES TO MAGNETS*. Mt.Rainier, MD: Gryphon House, 1990. ISBN 0-87659-150-0

Sisson, Edith A. *NATURE WITH CHILDREN OF ALL AGES*. New York: Prentice Hall Press, 1982. ISBN 0-13-611542-X

Smithsonian Institution. *MORE SCIENCE ACTIVITIES*. New York: GMG Publishing, 1988.
ISBN 0-939456-16-8

Thomas, Anne Wall. *COLORS FROM THE EARTH*. New York: Van Nostrand Reinhold Company, 1980. ISBN 0-442-25786-4

Tofts, Hannah. *THE PAPER BOOK*. New York: Simon and Schuster Books for Young Readers, 1990. ISBN 0-671-70357-6

Vermeer, Jackie and Lariviere, Marian. *THE LITTLE KIDS CRAFT BOOK*. New York: Taplinger Publishing Company, 1973. ISBN 0-8008-4459-8

Wagpole, Brenda. *175 SCIENCE EXPERIMENTS*. New York: Random House Inc., 1988.
ISBN 0-394-89991-1

Warren, Jean. *123 ART*. Everett, WA: Warren Publishing House, Inc., 1985. ISBN 0-911019-06-5

Wilmes, Liz and Dick. *EXPLORING ART*. Elgin, IL: Building Blocks, 1986. ISBN 0-943452-05-8

Wiseman, Ann. *MAKING THINGS*. Boston: Little, Brown and Company, 1973.
ISBN 0-316-94849-7

# PROJECTS INDEX

# MATERIALS INDEX

The Materials Index can be helpful in several ways:

1.  Use as a checklist to see which projects match up with materials and supplies you already have or can easily find.

2.  Use as a guide for materials to compile for future art experiences.

3.  When you remember a material you've used in a project, but not the name of the project, use the Index to find that project and its page number.
**NOTE:** Basic supplies such as scissors, glue, paper, and paint are not listed unless used as a unique or unusual part of the art experience.

222 — resource guide

## ABOUT THE AUTHORS

**MaryAnn F. Kohl** graduated from Old Dominion University, Virginia, with a BS in Elementary Education, and graduate studies at Western Washington State University. Her interest in creative art for children comes from years of teaching elementary and preschool aged children, using a whole language and learning center approach. Most recently she has worked as an educational consultant in art, illustrating, and publishing for young authors. MaryAnn also enjoys skiing, boating, and being a mom. She lives with her husband and two daughters in Bellingham, Washington.

**Cindy Gainer** has a BFA from Seaton Hill College, Pennsylvania, in Art and Education with graduate work in art for children. She has taught art in public and private schools in southwestern Pennsylvania to kids age 5 through 18. Cindy also illustrates children's books. In addition to writing, illustrating, and teaching, Cindy enjoys running, playing guitar, and singing. She lives in Jeannette, PA, with her husband Bill and son August.

# ORDER FORM

**Bright Ring Publishing**

P.O. Box 5768 • Bellingham, WA 98227
(206) 734-1601 / FAX (206) 676-1271
800-480-4ART for orders

Name_____

Address_____

City_____ State____ Zip_____

Phone: (____)_____

| Qty. | Title of Book | Price Each | Price |
|------|---------------|-----------|-------|
| | SCRIBBLE ART *Independent Creative Art for Children* | $14.95 | |
| | MUDWORKS *Creative Clay, Dough and Modeling* | $14.95 | |
| | GOOD EARTH ART *Environmental Art for Kids* | $16.95 | |
| | SCIENCE ARTS *Discovering Science Through Art Experiences* | $15.95 | |
| | PRESCHOOL ART *It's the Process Not the Product* | $19.95 | |
| | Total for books | | |
| | Deduct 10% for orders of 4 or more books | | |
| | SUBTOTAL | | |
| | Sales Tax @ 7.8% (Washington only) | | |
| | Shipping (see chart) | | |
| | **TOTAL ENCLOSED** | | |

Please make checks payable to:
Bright Ring Publishing.

## SHIPPING CHART

USPS Book Rate, 4th Class:
$2.50 – 1st Book          $1.00 – each additional

UPS and AirMail:
$4.00 – 1st book          $2.00 – each additional

Orders shipped within 3 business days.
Allow 2 weeks for shipment to arrive.

# 🙂 BRIGHT IDEAS BOOKSHELF

Bright Ring Publishing encourages the creative ability of each child by producing quality art idea books that inspire exploration and discovery through art process. We like to say, "Process not Product!" because the process of creating and exploring art is more important than the final product. All of the books in our Bright Ideas for Learning series build upon the natural curiosity and creativity of children of all ages. Everyone can be an artist.

MAK   MaryAnn Kohl ♡
publisher and author

### ALL NEW

**SCRIBBLE ART**
*Independent Creative Art Experiences for Children*
(originally published as SCRIBBLE COOKIES)

11x8-1/2 • 160 pages • $14.95 • paperback
ISBN 0-935607-05-6

Over 200 process art ideas that stress exploration in an independent, non-competitive, open-ended setting. Activities need only basic art supplies and common kitchen materials. Three Indexes, charted Table of Contents, child-tested activities. Ideal for any age, for home, school, or child care.

❖ 1991 Daycare Directors Choice Award ❖

**MUDWORKS**
*Creative Clay, Dough, and Modeling Experiences*

11x8-1/2 • 152 pages • $14.95 • paperback
ISBN 0-935607-02-1

Anyone who likes to play in mud, playdough, papier-mache and similar mediums will love this book of over 125 clays, doughs, and modeling mixtures. Uses common household materials and requires no expertise. Ideal for fun or serious art for all ages, for home, school, or child care.

❖ 1991 Benjamin Franklin Award ❖
❖ 1990 American Library Assn. Starred Review ❖

**SCIENCE ARTS**
*Discovering Science Through Art Experiences*

11x8-1/2 • 144 pages • $15.95 • paperback
ISBN 0-935607-04-8

Children 3-10 learn basic science concepts as they explore over 200 amazing and beautiful art experiences using common household materials. Projects are open-ended and easy to do. One science-art experiment per page, fully illustrated. Includes three indexes and a charted Table of Contents. Suitable for home, school, or child care.

❖ 1994 Benjamin Franklin Award ❖
❖ 1994 National Press Communicator Award ❖

**GOOD EARTH ART**
*Environmental Art For Kids*

11x8-1/2 • 224 pages • $16.95 • paperback
ISBN 0-935607-01-3

Over 200 art projects that develop an awareness of the environment and a caring attitude towards the earth. Uses common materials collected from nature or recycled from trash. Filled with simple ideas to recycle and create for all ages. Includes charted Table of Contents, two indexes, and a list of environmental resources.

❖ 1992 Benjamin Franklin Award ❖

**PRESCHOOL ART**
*It's the Process Not the Product*

11x8-1/2 • 260 pages • $19.95 • paperback
ISBN 0-87659-168-3

Over 250 process-oriented art experiences designed for children 3-6, but ideal for all ages. Uses materials commonly found in the home or school. Organized by months and seasons. Index. Published by Gryphon House, Inc., Beltsville, MD.